MARCH OF EMPIRE

MARCH OF EMPIRE
The European Overseas Possessions on the Eve of the First World War

By
Lowell Ragatz, F.R.H.S.
Professor of European History
in The George Washington University

Foreword by Alfred Martineau

H. L. LINDQUIST
New York

325.3
g R128m

Nov. 9, 1948
Max. Hist.

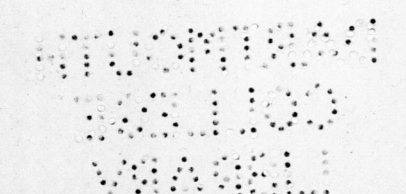

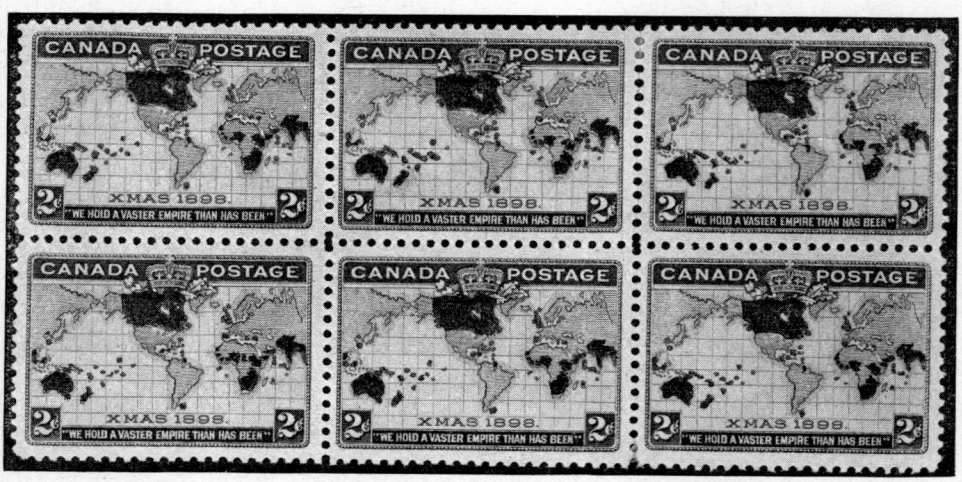

**THE CANADIAN CHRISTMAS STAMP OF 1898,
THE EPITOME OF MODERN IMPERIALISM.**

The phrase, "We hold a vaster empire than has been," is excerpted from *Jubilee Ode*, by the Welsh poet, Sir Lewis Morris (1833-1907).

Copyright, 1948

By

Lowell Ragatz

PRINTED IN THE UNITED STATES OF AMERICA

To
Chuko and Pancho Liang,
Dear Friends of Long Ago

FOREWORD

The period from the Fashoda Crisis to the outbreak of the great World War in 1914 has been generally neglected by specialists in European expansion. It is as though the several colonial empires had become static entities upon the close of the 19th century and that nothing of consequence had transpired in any of them in the decade and a half prior to the outbreak of that global struggle marking the end of an era in Modern Imperialism. Nothing is, of course, farther from the truth.

I have, therefore, suggested to my former student and present colleague in the field of colonial studies, Professor Lowell Ragatz, of The George Washington University in the United States, that he write a small volume filling this singular gap in the writings on modern empire building. This he has now done, in a manner eminently suited to meet existing needs.

The appended bibliography is a highly selective one, extracted from his comprehensive *Literature of European Imperialism, 1815-1939,* now in press in America. The former will meet the needs of the general reader; the latter will prove invaluable for the scholar and the research student.

Thanks are due the Graduate Council of The George Washington University for generous financial assistance in preparing the manuscript and seeing the volume through the press.

ALFRED MARTINEAU,
Sometime Professor of Colonial History in the College de France; Editor, Revue d'Histoire des Colonies.

LIST OF ILLUSTRATIONS

The Canadian Christmas Stamp of 1898, Epitome of Modern Imperialism.........Frontispiece

After Page

1	The British Empire in 1914.	4
2	The French Empire in 1914.	28
3	The German and Portuguese Empires in 1914.	42
4	The Italian Empire in 1914.	52
5	The Dutch and Danish Empires in 1914.	56
6	The Belgian and Spanish Empires in 1914.	60
7	The Russian Empire in 1914.	64
8	The Railroads of Africa in 1914.	66
9	The Railroads of Asia in 1914.	68
10	Tropical Commodities Production Areas in 1914.	70

All maps were specially drawn for this work by Walter Y. Cox.

Contents

Chapter		Page
	Foreword, by Alfred Martineau	v
I	The Background	1
II	The British Empire	4
	Africa	4
	The Union of South Africa	4
	The South African Protectorates	6
	Bechuanaland	6
	Basutoland	6
	Swaziland	7
	Rhodesia	7
	Nyasaland	7
	Egypt and the Soudan	8
	British East Africa	10
	Uganda Protectorate	11
	Zanzibar	12
	British Somaliland	12
	Nigeria	12
	Gold Coast	13
	Sierra Leone	14
	Gambia	15
	America	15
	Canada	15
	Newfoundland	17
	Bermuda and the Caribbean Colonies	17
	The Falkland Islands	18
	Asia	19
	India	19
	Ceylon	20
	Malaya	21
	The Enclaves	21
	Aden	21
	Hong Kong	22
	Weihaiwei	22
	The Indian Ocean Islands	22
	Australasia	23
	The Commonwealth of Australia	23
	New Zealand	24

Chapter		Page
	Oceania	25
	Territorial Readjustments	25
	Economic Development	25
	The Mediterranean "Life-Line"	26
	Great Britain	26
III	The French Empire	28
	Africa	28
	French North Africa (Maghreb)	28
	Algeria	28
	Tunis	29
	Morocco	30
	French West Africa ("A.O.F.")	32
	French Equatorial Africa ("A.E.F.")	33
	French Somaliland	34
	Madagascar	35
	Reunion	35
	America	36
	St. Pierre and Miquelon	36
	Guadeloupe and Martinique	36
	French Guiana	36
	Asia	37
	The French Establishments in India	37
	Indochina	37
	Oceania	38
	France	39
IV	The German Colonial Empire	41
	Africa	41
	Togoland	41
	Kamerun	41
	German Southwest Africa	42
	German East Africa	43
	Asia	43
	The Pacific Basin	44
	Germany	45
V	The Portuguese Empire	47
	Africa	47
	St. Thomas and Prince's Islands	47
	Guinea	47
	Angola	48
	Portuguese East Africa	48
	Asia	49
	Portugal	49
VI	The Italian Empire	51
	Africa	51
	Eritrea	51
	Somaliland	51
	Tripolitania and Cyrenaica	52
	Italy	54

Chapter		Page
VII	The Dutch Empire	56
	The Caribbean Area	56
	Netherlands India	56
	The Netherlands	57
VIII	The Danish Empire	58
	America	58
	Iceland	58
	Greenland	58
	The Danish West Indies	59
	Denmark	59
IX	The Belgian Empire	60
	The Belgian Congo	60
	Belgium	62
X	The Spanish Empire	63
	Aftermath of the American War	63
	Africa	63
	Western Sahara	63
	Spanish Guinea	63
	Spanish Morocco	64
	Spain	64
XI	The Russian Empire	65
	The Far East	65
	The Middle East	66
	Russia	68
XII	Trends in European Expansion, 1898-1914	69
	Select Bibliography	71

Chapter I

The Background

THE heroic age of European expansion was drawing to a close by the turn of the twentieth century. Between 1492 and 1900 the occidental peoples discovered and colonized the Americas, Australasia and Oceania, and laid claim to vast regions in Africa and Asia as well. More than a hundred million Europeans sought new homes overseas in those four hundred years. One third that number emigrated in the nineteenth century; twenty million left British ports alone from 1815 to 1900. This was the greatest folk movement of all time. It peopled the new world, Australia and New Zealand, and introduced a large western strain into the other continents and the Pacific Basin. Wherever they went, the Europeans took their languages, customs, ideals and civilization with them. By 1900 they dominated the world economically, politically and culturally.

The Americas, the Indian Peninsula and the East Indies were the chief theaters of international rivalry through the eighteenth century. A temporary lull followed the disruption of the French, British, Portuguese and Spanish Empires which occurred between the outbreak of the Seven Years' War (1756) and the close of the Hispanic American Wars of Independence (1825). For a full half century thereafter, interest in overseas expansion stood at low ebb. Even Disraeli (1804-1881), destined to become the personification of British imperialism, then branded colonies millstones around any country's neck. A sudden revival of interest followed in the 1870's because of the rapid industrialization of Europe, the widespread erection of tariff barriers and the demands of business for new supplies of raw products and enlarged markets.

David Livingstone (1813-1873) and Henry Stanley (1841-1904) had revealed the fabulous wealth of Africa. A rush to stake out claims now set in, and between 1875 and 1900 the partition of Africa was effected. Great Britain and France, leading colonial powers of an earlier day, again played prominent roles in that gigantic real estate transaction. Three countries hitherto inactive in overseas enterprise—Belgium, Italy and Germany—likewise acquired extensive holdings, while Portugal succeeded in converting coastal footholds into magnificent domains. At Adowa in 1896, while attempting to conquer Ethiopia, Italy suffered the most crushing defeat experienced by any European power in the history of modern imperialism. Rivalry in Africa contributed materially to the mounting hostility between

Great Britain and Germany, while the Fashoda Crisis of 1898, arising out of French hopes for incorporating the Soudan within a vast east-west empire despite British claims to the region, precipitated a major diplomatic conflict and threatened a modern contest of herculean proportions between these ancient foes.

By the late 1890's, with most parts of the African continent under European control, the movement subsided. It was followed by an era of consolidation in which conflicting claims were adjusted, hinterland boundaries were drawn and the exploitation of resources got under way on a large scale. The remaining lands were largely conquered by 1914. Thus it came about that, whereas nearly sixty per cent of Africa had been independent in 1875, only Ethiopia and Liberia, comprising 3.5 per cent of the continent, enjoyed that status on the eve of the World War. Great Britain's holdings had risen from 580,000 square miles to 2,125,000 in the interim; France's from 1,500,000 sq. m. to 4,250,000 and Spain's from 10,800 sq. m. to 129,000. Germany, Belgium and Italy, which had no African possessions in 1875, held title to 1,100,000 sq. m., 900,000 sq. m. and 865,000 sq. m. of territory respectively in 1914.

The first three-quarters of the nineteenth century witnessed steady British gains in Hindustan. British East India Company rule gave way to Crown control in 1858 and the Indian Empire was created in 1877. Russia acquired the trans-Amur region and the Maritime Province from China and made extensive gains in the Caspian area by the conquest of native states in this same period. Then, because of the sudden revival of interest in expansion throughout Europe after 1875, a scramble for Asiatic lands ensued, with Great Britain, Russia, France and Germany participating. Because of the higher state of development in Asia, annexations there were fewer than in Africa, and were, for the most part, made at the expense of Siam, China and small native states. Spheres of interest were carved out of Asiatic Turkey and Persia. The movement reached its apogee in a mass assault on China and the forced leasing of strategic ports to foreign powers. Dismemberment of the Celestial Empire was, however, halted by the United States which evolved the Open Door Policy to safeguard its commercial interests in the Far East.

Imperialistic rivalry in the period 1875-1900 gave birth to bitter feeling between Russia and Japan, which had become westernized and was now turning covetous eyes to the adjacent mainland. It likewise engendered animosity between Russia and the British, who grew increasingly alarmed over the Muscovite approach to India. These hostilities profoundly influenced the course of international relations in the pre-war decade.

Great Britain's Asiatic holdings rose from 1,850,000 square miles in 1875 to 1,970,000 in 1914 and France's from 96,500 sq. m. to 285,000. The Spanish American War, which abruptly terminated Spain's hold on the Philippines, unexpectedly gave the United States Far Eastern interests and revolutionized its foreign policy. The Netherlands played no part in these events but continued to hold the East Indian archipelago where she had established herself in the seventeenth century.

Most of Oceania had already been brought under European control by 1875—less than six per cent of the whole then remained independent. Great Britain, Germany and the United States acquired the remainder by 1900. The first increased its possessions there by 100,000 square miles through occupation and international agreement. Annexation, coupled with the purchase of what remained of Spanish Oceania following the Spanish-American War, gave Germany, which had no Pacific holdings in 1875, possession of 90,000 sq. m. at the close of the nineteenth century. The United States, through the conquest of Guam and the Philippines and the annexation of Hawaii and Samoa, now held 120,000 sq. m. French territory continued stationary at 10,000 sq. m. The Spanish flag had, at the same time, disappeared from the Pacific.

Thus, by the opening of the twentieth century, the days of large-scale conquest were over. Save for the Americas the world was chiefly in European hands and little opportunity remained for territorial gains save at another power's expense. But the Old World nations no longer trod the path of empire alone. The United States, just become a major state, was now, for the first time in its history, in possession of outlying dependencies and thus found itself directly involved in Far Eastern and Pacific affairs. Japan, an oriental nation which was developing territorial ambitions of its own, was determined to realize them in western fashion through conflict with Russia, an expanding occidental power. These new factors could not fail profoundly to influence the course of overseas developments in the early 1900's.

Imperialist sentiment, too, was running high at this time. Entire nations were now conscious of their imperial destinies, and save for the Socialists, who adhered to their creed of human brotherhood, Europeans generally evinced keen pride in the pomp and circumstance of empire. Their visions of grandeur were, however, accompanied by an impelling missionary urge to bear "The White Man's Burden." Kipling's immortal poem of that title, with its flamboyant assertion of western superiority and its emphasis upon the occidental's solemn obligation to carry the blessings of Christian civilization to less-favored peoples, was a natural product of the age.

CHAPTER II

The British Empire
AFRICA

THE UNION OF SOUTH AFRICA

THE opening of the twentieth century found Great Britain in the throes of the Boer War. The British had sadly underrated their antagonists and were caught unawares by the outbreak of hostilities. The Boers at once besieged Kimberley and Mafeking in Cape Colony and Ladysmith in Natal. Colonial forces proved inadequate, and a British army under General Redvers Buller (1839-1908) was rushed to their rescue. When the latter failed to lift the sieges, he was superseded by Field Marshal Roberts (1832-1914) with Major General Kitchener (1850-1916) as Chief of Staff. The transport system was reorganized, and on February 15, 1900 Kimberley was relieved.

Catastrophe now overwhelmed the Boers. On February 27 a Transvaal army under General Piet Cronje (1840?-1911) capitulated at Paardeberg. Besieging forces were driven from Ladysmith a month later. Bloemfontein, capital of the Orange Free State, was captured on March 13. The siege of Mafeking was lifted on May 17 and the Free State was annexed on May 28. Johannesburg, at the center of the gold fields, fell on the 31st and Pretoria, the Transvaal capital, on June 5. Annexation of the republic followed in October. Petrus Joubert (1834-1900), Commander-in-Chief of the Boer forces, died in the midst of these disasters and the Transvaal President, Paul Kruger (1825-1904), fled to Europe in a vain effort to enlist foreign support. With the war apparently over, Roberts departed for England leaving Kitchener to liquidate affairs.

Though beaten in the open field, the Boers were by no means conquered and the conflict now entered upon its second, more protracted phase. The Boer army was dispersed by General Louis Botha (1863-1919), its new head, and was replaced by commandos which launched guerrilla warfare. Small bands headed by Jacobus de la Rey (1847-1914), James Hertzog (1866-1942), Christian Beyers (1869-1914), Christian de Wet (1854-1922) and Botha harassed the British for eighteen months. Cape Colony was invaded early in 1901. Large numbers of Cape Boers likewise revolted and placed themselves under Jan Smuts (1870-   ), a Cape-born Transvaaler.

The British were helpless in the face of such tactics. In 1901, on the arrival of

1914

Swaziland

Swaziland, which had passed under Transvaal's domination in 1894, threw its support to Great Britain in the Boer War. The latter assumed provisional control on the restoration of peace, and in 1906 set up a protectorate. Sobhuza II, a boy of eight, was chosen ruler and was educated in an English school while his grandmother served as regent.

Some 240,000 acres were assigned to the natives. The rest of the area, claimed as Crown land, was placed on the market. Immigration was, however, slight. There were merely 1,250 Europeans resident in 1914, engaged chiefly in ranching. Cattle, sheep, hides and wool were the chief exports. Cotton and tobacco cultivation had been introduced but were still in their infancy while gold and tin mining had barely begun. In 1910 this territory, too, entered the South African Customs Union.

RHODESIA

Rhodesia made rapid strides following the close of the Boer War. British South Africa Company officials continued to view the corporation's activities as an imperial trust. Cecil Rhodes' (b. 1853) procedure of employing all earnings in further development was followed after his death in 1902 and no dividends were ever declared.

Railway construction was pushed and direct communication between lower Rhodesia and the Cape opened in 1902. The Zambezi was bridged at Victoria Falls in 1905 and the Congo frontier had almost been reached by 1914.

The white population rose from 10,000 to 35,000 between 1900 and the World War. Immigrants were chiefly well-to-do Britishers who opened ranches or mines. Liberalization of the land laws in 1907 gave marked impetus to agriculture. While settlers tended to concentrate below the Zambezi, the exploitation of lands to the north dates from this period. Boundary disputes with Portugal were adjusted in 1905. Gold, chrome ore, livestock and tobacco became the chief export items. Foreign trade reached £7,000,000 by 1913, with exports and imports almost balanced, mirroring the area's rapid economic advance.

Upon creation of the South African Union in 1910, provision was made for the voluntary entry of Rhodesia into the dominion at a later date. Expiration of the Company's charter in 1914 made some action imperative, but the Boer nationalist movement occasioned grave apprehension in Britain and self-government for Rhodesia came to be viewed as the only feasible solution. The charter was, consequently, renewed for ten years with the understanding that corporation rule should terminate within that time and the discussion of moot points, such as the ownership of unalienated land and the corporation's future status in the area, opened.

NYASALAND

The British Central African Protectorate was administered by Sir Alfred Sharpe from 1897 to 1910. Due to lack of transportation, development was exceedingly slow. High freight charges precluded the exportation of an abundance of tropical products and cotton, tea, coffee and tobacco were the only crops grown. Herds were decimated by sleeping sickness and the region suffered a sharp setback in consequence. There was little immigration and in 1913 there were only 758 whites in the country. Natives increased steadily in number owing to tribal movements from Mozambique.

The Colonial Office assumed control in 1904. White residents were given a voice in affairs three years later and a new name, Nyasaland, was adopted at the same time. Foreign trade rose from £255,000 to £475,000 between 1900 and 1914.

EGYPT AND THE SOUDAN

The political status of the Nile valley at the turn of the century was highly anomalous. Egypt was technically a tributary province of the Turkish Empire governed by a native dynasty. It had, however, been under British military occupation since 1882 and was, in all but name, a British protectorate. The Soudan had been conquered by Egyptian forces during the 1820's, had been lost in the 1880's, and had been reconquered by a joint Anglo-Egyptian expedition under Kitchener in 1898. A condominium had been created a year later. The fact that the Suez Canal cut across Egypt made the latter extremely valuable from the strategic point of view. The Soudan was prized because it controlled the headwaters of the Nile on which Egypt's prosperity rested.

Abbas Hilmi (1874-1944), the Egyptian khedive, was merely titular ruler. Actual power rested in the hands of Lord Cromer (1841-1917), British Consul-General and Agent, one of the greatest proconsuls of modern times. In sixteen years he had re-established order in Egypt, regained control of the Soudan, rehabilitated Egyptian finances, brought enormous tracts of fertile land under cultivation through irrigation, placed taxes on a rational basis and suppressed slavery and forced labor. National credit had been restored and the Egyptian people were enjoying material prosperity for the first time in centuries. Cromer was, in every sense, the maker of modern Egypt. As he stood behind Abbas, directing the executive's every act, so other Englishmen stood behind all Egyptian officials in responsible posts, performing the actual duties of office. The British did not govern Egypt; rather, they governed its Government.

There was, however, vigorous opposition from two quarters. The French, who had declined to participate in the occupation of 1882, vented their wrath at the turn of events intrenching the British by embarrassing them on all conceivable occasions. Their virulence after Fashoda occasioned grave concern. A nationalist movement headed by Mustafa Kamil (1874-1908) was likewise gaining headway among the rising generation which had not experienced the iniquities of the old regime. *The Egyptian Standard* served as its organ. This scurrilous sheet, published in Paris with financial assistance from the French Government, sought to discredit the British by innuendo, perversion and falsehood and incited bitter hostility against them.

A change came in 1904 when Great Britain and France reversed history by patching up their quarrels in face of the common German menace and negotiated the Entente Cordiale. In return for a free hand in Morocco, France now accorded her traditional enemy a free hand in Egypt. Germany, Austria and Italy shortly after recognized Britain's dominant position in the country. By international agreement, Egypt at the same time regained financial independence, which she had lost in the 1870's. The capitulations, granting immunities to numerous national groups, continued in force until 1937.

These events greatly strengthened the nationalist cause. Though no longer enjoying French support, anti-British agitation was now abetted by Turkish patriots seeking to restore the Ottoman Empire and became intimately associated with pan-Islamism. The nationalists, however, aimed at the abolition of both British and Turkish control and Zaghlul Pasha (1850?-1927), Mustafa Kamil's successor, announced complete independence as their goal. Two incidents occurring in 1906 inflamed nationalist passions. Turkish authorities suddenly occupied the Egyptian frontier port of Taba and refused to withdraw until confronted by a British ultimatum. Villagers, setting upon British officers shooting native pigeons at Denshawai in June, were accorded such drastic punishment that the entire country was aroused. Though personally hostile to nationalist leaders, Abbas, too, became increasingly restive at this time and proved far less cooperative than in the past.

Cromer's resignation in April 1907, due to ill health, was followed by grave complications. His successor, Sir Eldon Gorst (1861-1911), who had long been financial adviser to the khedive, inaugurated a policy of increased local self-government. The Egyptian Parliament met this concession with a demand for independence and the nationalist majority in 1910 repudiated a proposal to extend the Canal Company's charter. Boutros Pasha, the Christian premier who had worked in harmony with the British, was assassinated by a youthful patriot immediately after. On Gorst's retirement in July 1911, with death but a few weeks removed, the country was in chaos.

General Kitchener was now named to the post in an effort to rebuild British prestige. Order was quickly restored. A drastic usury law to safeguard the peasantry against exploitation was enacted. Parliament was reorganized in 1913 and its powers were broadened. The nationalists, however, controlled it from the outset and elected Zaghlul Pasha vice-president. A plot to assassinate both Abbas and Kitchener was, happily, frustrated. Personal relations between the two men were strained from the outset. Abbas sought to regain the lost powers of the early khediviate and became deeply enmeshed in intrigue. Kitchener alternately sought to browbeat and to conciliate him and made little headway. To complicate the situation, legislative action was blocked by obstructionist tactics and Parliament frittered away months on trivialities.

The outbreak of war in 1914 ended this stalemate. Parliament was prorogued, government by decree was legalized through the proclamation of martial law and, following Turkey's entry into the conflict, a British protectorate was established on December 18. Khedive Abbas Hilmi was deposed and his uncle, Husein Kamel (d. 1917), was placed on the throne with the new title of Sultan. Thus, at length, after 32 years of military occupation, the British position in the country was regularized.

Egypt's population rose from 9,750,000 to 11,200,000 between 1897 and 1913. Its foreign trade soared from £E 30,750,000 in 1900 to £E 60,000,000 in 1913. Under British financial control, all interest payments were made on schedule and the foreign debt was steadily decreased through amortization. By 1914 economic strain had been eased and the country's financial structure was in order.

While the Soudan was nominally a condominium and Egypt shared the cost of its defense and rule, Great Britain in reality enjoyed complete control. The Governor-General was nominated by the British Government and was, of course, a British subject. Provincial executives and administrative heads were likewise British nationals and only minor posts fell to the Egyptians. Sir Francis Wingate (1861-   ), Governor-General from 1899-1916, was the Soudanese Cromer. He restored order, abolished the slave trade, conciliated the natives by preserving their laws and customs, fostered agriculture and commerce and curbed missionary ardor. Regular steamer service and extensive railroad construction facilitated marketing. The line from Atbara on the Nile to Port Soudan on the Red Sea shortened haulage to the sea by 750 miles. Ranching and the gum arabic trade, in particular, flourished. Cotton cultivation, today a leading industry, was well under way by 1914. Foreign trade reached £E 3,185,000 by 1913. The Sennar and Gebel Aulia dams, which will ultimately water 3.25 million acres of land, were projected that year. On the outbreak of the First World War the country was prosperous and a bright future was envisaged.

BRITISH EAST AFRICA

The interior plateau-land of British East Africa was well-suited for European settlement but its development hinged upon transportation. This was at length provided by the Uganda Railway, the main portion of which traversed the protectorate from Mombasa to Lake Victoria, and which was completed in 1901 at a cost of nearly £5,500,000 borne by the British Treasury.

Immigrants at once appeared in considerable number, and by 1914 there were 4,000 whites in the country. These were chiefly of South African and British extraction. Sharp conflict raged in 1903-1904 between speculators seeking large grants and actual settlers wishing to take up small tracts. Sir Charles Eliot (1854-   ), the Commissioner, championed the latter in an acrimonious controversy with Lord Lansdowne (1845-1927), the Secretary of State for Foreign Affairs, his superior. The settlers ultimately triumphed but not until after Eliot resigned rather than lease a syndicate 500 sq. m. of the best land on Lansdowne's orders (1904). An offer of 6,000 sq. m. to the Zionist Association was declined but, by the spring of 1905, when control over the protectorate was shifted from the Foreign Office to the Colonial Office, 1,000,000 acres had been alienated. The rule of sale to natives and leases to all others was now put into operation. Grants were also limited by law and were voided unless stipulated improvements were carried through within a reasonably short time.

The native problem proved a thorny one. Home authorities viewed the protection of African rights as a sacred duty. Choice lands were set aside as reserves and the use of colored labor was hedged by innumerable restrictions. This was much resented by all white settlers. Certain tribes, such as the Nandi of the southwest, still gave their predatory instincts free rein and in 1905 it proved necessary to subjugate them. Incessant depredations likewise engendered bitter hostility. The color question came to a head in 1911 when the Honorable Galbraith Cole, a distinguished colonist who had killed a native caught in sheep theft, was deported. No solution had been found by the opening of the World War.

White and Hindu relations were likewise bad. The Indians had entered as coolies during the era of railroad construction. By 1914 they outnumbered the whites three to one. Through underselling the latter, whose higher standard of living demanded larger profits, they had come into virtual control of the native trade. They were segregated in the towns and, by decision of the Colonial Office in 1908, their agricultural operations were restricted to the hot lowlands. Such discrimination awakened fierce resentment in India.

The post of Commissioner was elevated to a Governorship in 1906. Sir Percy Girouard, holding office from 1909 to 1912, proved an exceptionally capable executive and under his benign rule the protectorate for the first time paid its own way.

Up to 1907 the colonists had no voice in affairs. When, however, an appointed Legislative Council was set up in that year, they were accorded four seats out of twelve. This failed to satisfy them and the Colonists' Association, headed by Lord Delamere, carried on unceasing agitation for increased participation in government.

Grain, sisal, cattle, cotton and coffee were the chief products. Exports, which stood at £110,000 at the turn of the century, rose to ten times that figure by the eve of the War and imports showed a corresponding increase.

UGANDA PROTECTORATE

With the crushing of the great native rebellion in 1899, the pacification of Uganda Protectorate was completed. King Mwanga (d. 1903) of Buganda, the leading state, was deposed in favor of his infant son, Daudi Chwa, and the country was governed by regents until 1914. These notables accorded the British hearty cooperation and their example was followed by the rulers of adjoining territories. Sir Harry Johnston (1858-1927) was named Commissioner in 1899. He abolished slavery and introduced modern administrative procedure as well as private land tenure before his departure two years later. Completion of the Uganda Railroad (under construction from 1895-1901) and inauguration of steamer service on Lake Victoria in this period obviated the protracted Nile journey and placed the country in easy communication with the outer world.

In 1903 two southeastern provinces along upper Lake Victoria, embracing the western terminal of the Uganda Railway, were yielded to British East Africa. Boundary rectifications carried through with the Belgian Congo and the Soudan in 1912 and 1914 respectively, ultimately gave Uganda an area of 110,000 square miles.

Rapid economic advance followed completion of the railway. Immigrants by 1913 included 823 whites and 3,100 Hindus. Wild rubber formed an important export item until the supply was depleted about 1910. Ivory and hides were likewise shipped out in abundance. Cotton was the sole pre-war plantation product and after 1910 headed the list of exports. The latter rose from £50,000 in 1901 to £457,000 in 1912-1913 and imports from £190,000 in 1904 to £780,000 in 1912-13. Development was, however, seriously hampered by sleeping sickness which claimed 300,000 natives between 1901 and 1914.

The Colonial Office assumed control in 1906. Sir Hesketh Bell (1864-   ) was named first Governor. He viewed Uganda as an African domain, made native interests his primary concern and protected the blacks against immigrant encroachment. The British regime brought prosperity and on the eve of war the tribesmen's economic status was enviable. The protectorate became self-supporting in 1915.

ZANZIBAR

The Zanzibar Protectorate, embracing the islands of Zanzibar and Pemba and a ten-mile deep coastal strip between Italian Somaliland and German East Africa, enjoyed great prosperity during pre-war years. Clove planting in the insular territories increased steadily and in 1914 production surpassed four-fifths the world supply. Wide demand sent the price from 4½ d. a lb. in 1899 to 11 d. in 1914 and all elements profited by the rise. The development of British East Africa and Uganda fostered the growth of Mombasa, the eastern terminus of the Uganda Railroad, and by 1914 it already overshadowed Zanzibar City. The latter, however, continued a great port and a warehousing center. Exports in 1913 stood at £1,050,000 and imports at £1,100,000, both substantially the same as in 1900.

The 100,000 slaves accorded emancipation in 1897 were slow to claim their independence. While bondage was officially proclaimed extinct in 1907, compensation for their former masters' protection was allowed ex-slaves up to 1911. Grave social and economic problems raised by the destruction of the thriving trade in blacks and the introduction of free paid labor were still far from solved by 1914.

The protectorate passed under the Colonial Office's jurisdiction in 1913. The Governor of British East Africa thereafter likewise served as High Commissioner of Zanzibar.

BRITISH SOMALILAND

Grave disorders commencing in 1899 rent the protectorate for many years. These arose from the activities of Mohammed bin Abdullah (d. 1921), "the mad mullah", a puritanical religious leader who proclaimed himself the Islamic Messiah and proved bitterly hostile to alien control. Repeated attempts to crush him failed and the British withdrew from the interior in 1910. The greater part of the country was in his hands until 1920 when, with the aid of aerial forces, his power was at length broken and he was driven into exile. Adequate surveys were first made in conjunction with the numerous campaigns launched against him.

The country stagnated throughout this period. Hides, gum and ostrich feathers were the chief exports. Construction of the Djibuti-Addis Ababa Railway largely destroyed the old carrying trade between British Somaliland and Ethiopia. Imports in 1912-1913 stood at £250,000 and exports at £230,000. Control was transferred from the Foreign to the Colonial Office in 1905.

NIGERIA

The early years of the twentieth century witnessed a consolidation of British interests in the Niger valley. To the east, along the Guinea shore, lay the Niger Coast Protectorate (formerly the Oil Rivers Protectorate); to the west, Lagos Colony and Protectorate; and in the interior the domains of the Royal Niger Company. Fears respecting German and French designs led the British Government to relieve the Company of political responsibility on January 1, 1900 and the latter thereafter concerned itself solely with economic affairs. The corporation's former domains, lying below approximately 7° north of the equator, and Niger Coast Protectorate were, at the same time, amalgamated to form the Protectorate of Southern Nigeria, while lands to the north became the Northern Nigeria Protectorate. The Colonial Office now assumed control of the two Lagoses and both Nigerias. Pacification of Southern Nigeria was completed in 1902, and in 1906 Lagos Colony, Lagos Protectorate and the Protectorate of South Nigeria were united to form the Colony and Protectorate of Southern Nigeria, with British officials exercising direct control in all branches of the administration.

This new political unit underwent rapid development. Palm oil, cotton and cacao were the chief products. A railroad, opened in Lagos in 1900, soon converted Lagos City, its southern terminal, into a leading West African metropolis. Port Harcourt was founded in 1914 as an outlet for recently-discovered coal fields. King's College was opened in Lagos City in 1909.

Northern Nigeria, on the contrary, was in a primitive state. Colonel Lugard (1858-   ), the first High Commissioner, was at the outset obliged to establish British authority. This involved crushing numerous emirs and their overlord, the Sultan of Sokoto, which was accomplished by 1903. Thereafter the Sultan and all chieftains were appointed by the British Government and indirect rule, with the cooperation of friendly native authorities, was inaugurated. Slavery was abolished but local law and custom were otherwise fully respected.

Under Sir Percy Girouard, the second High Commissioner (1907-1909), and Sir Hesketh Bell, Governor from 1909-1911, Northern Nigeria's status as a black man's country was fully established and the sale of land was prohibited in an effort to exclude white exploiters. Tin was discovered in 1902. Caravan routes were extended, wagon roads were constructed, river communication was improved and telegraph lines were erected. A railroad, opened in 1911, linked Kano, in the far north, and Baro, on the middle Niger, while an extension, joining the Lagos line, gave Northern Nigeria access to the sea. The boundary between the Protectorate and French West Africa and German Kamerun was defined in 1909.

Northern Nigeria's dependence upon Southern Nigeria, where its rail and river outlets lay, and its backward state provided strong arguments for amalgamating the two. As a preliminary step, Lugard was named Governor of both in 1912. He won native approval at a durbar attended by 63 of the leading chiefs and, on January 1, 1914, unification was effected. Lugard became first Governor-General of Nigeria Colony and Protectorate and filled this post with distinction until the close of the World War.

Trade for the entire area rose from £2,300,000 in 1900-1901 to £14,000,000 in 1913. All vegetable products were grown on native properties rather than on plantations. By the eve of the war, Nigeria was one of the best administered and prosperous colonial dependencies in the world—a striking example of modern imperialism at its best.

GOLD COAST

The defeat and exile of King Prempeh of Ashanti in 1900 led to the establishment of a protectorate over that kingdom a year later. Ashanti and Northern Territories Protectorate, lying immediately above and organized in 1897, were now both attached for administrative purposes to the Gold Coast Colony, along the Guinea littoral. These several units collectively formed Gold Coast Colony and Protectorate.

Construction of a railway between Sekondi, the chief port of Gold Coast, and Kumasi, the Ashanti capital, was completed in 1903 and knit the two states closely together. Communication with Northern Territories continued to rest upon unsatisfactory connections afforded by the temperamental Volta River and progress in that remote area was greatly retarded thereby.

Gold Coast and Ashanti, on the contrary, underwent phenomenal development. Systematic exploitation of the alluvial gold beds began in 1902 and yielded £800,000 a year by 1910. Manganese deposits were discovered on the eve of the war, but the prosperity of both areas rested upon agriculture rather than mining. The region became the world's chief source of supply for cacao in this period.

Exports soared from 350 tons worth £16,000 in 1899 to 50,000 tons valued at £2,500,000 by 1913. Wild rubber collection and coffee cultivation both became unprofitable because of the competition of Malayan and Brazilian plantations and now gave way to cacao and kola nut cultivation throughout the entire area. Production was exclusively in native hands and by 1914 prosperity was wide-spread. Imports rose from £1,290,000 in 1900 to £5,000,000 in 1913 and exports from £885,000 to £5,425,000 in the same years.

A technical school was opened at Accra, the capital, in 1909.

SIERRA LEONE

Sierra Leone Colony (a peninsula, several islands and a half-mile coastal strip) and Sierra Leone Protectorate (the back country, extending 180 miles inland, acquired in 1896) underwent rapid development between the turn of the century and the outbreak of the World War. An insurrection flared up in the Protectorate in 1898 in connection with an ill-advised attempt to abolish slavery. This was, however, soon suppressed and after the restoration of order the labor reform program was abandoned with the bizarre result that some 200,000 individuals continued in bondage until 1928 in an area originally brought within the British orbit as a haven of refuge for emancipated blacks.[1]

A 220 mile railway between Freetown and Baiama, opened in 1905, first gave access to the interior. Wild rubber exports were important for a time but sank as increased world production, resting upon plantation crops grown in Malaya and elsewhere, lowered the price, and palm oil, kola nuts and ginger, all produced by natives on their own small holdings, became the leading products before the War. The combined trade of Colony and Protectorate reached £2,750,000 in 1913 as compared with £920,000 in 1900.

To conciliate the natives, missionary activity was discouraged, Moslem educational institutions were opened in 1901 and a school for chieftains' sons was set up at Bo, in the Protectorate, in 1906. Preventive medicine and modern sanitation had done much by the eve of the War to destroy the region's sinister reputation as "the white man's grave."

---

[1] British humanitarians headed by William Wilberforce and Granville Sharp organized the Sierra Leone Company in 1791 to found a colony for liberated Negroes. The settlers were a rabble of ignorant freedmen landed amid hostile tribes demoralized by the slave trade, and this noble experiment ended in failure, with the British Government taking over in 1808.

GAMBIA

Gambia Colony (St. Mary's Island, with the port of Bathurst) and Gambia Protectorate (a 12-mile strip extending up the Gambia River for 250 miles) both suffered from being mere enclaves in French West Africa and having no hinterland to draw on. Yarbatenda, a settlement at the head of navigation, was ceded to France under the Entente Cordiale of 1904 in the hope that the Gambia River would be employed as an outlet for Senegal. Such expectations, however, proved illusory and little use continued to be made of this promising waterway. Much of the Protectorate's commerce was actually in French hands by 1914. France's acquisition of Gambia through an exchange of territory to round out her West African holdings was unofficially discussed in Paris but nothing came of the matter. French cooperation was secured in hunting down slave traders operating from Senegal and bondage was abolished in the Protectorate in 1906.

Peanuts, cultivated by the natives, formed the chief export item. Production in 1913 reached 50,000 tons. The trade of Colony and Protectorate combined rose from £600,000 in 1900 to £1,500,000 in 1914.

AMERICA

CANADA

The decade and a half before the First World War witnessed Canada's coming of age. With the closing of the frontier in the United States, the tide of European emigration turned northward and Americans in large number likewise sought opportunity in the Dominion. The population rose from 5,570,000 in 1901 to some 7,750,000 in 1913. Two million immigrants entered between 1906 and 1913, the number exceeding 400,000 in 1913 alone. The Prairie Provinces, in particular, profited by this mass migration. The population of Manitoba, Saskatchewan and Alberta trebled during the decade 1901-1911 and reached 1,300,000 by the latter year.

Americans formed the largest group of newcomers, outnumbering British immigrants two to one. In 1905 they took up nearly one-third of the 30,000 new homesteads entered that year, and ultimately became the predominant element in Saskatchewan and Alberta. The English, on the other hand, dominated British Columbia. Ukrainians and Doukhobars (pacifists leading a communal life under Peter Veregin, their leader) likewise came to Western Canada from Russia in village groups. In an effort to settle vacant lands beyond the Great Lakes, upwards of $1,000,000 a year was paid colonization agents abroad. Passage was, however, never provided, and the Government made no loans of money, stock or implements.

While oriental immigration (principally into British Columbia) raised the Chinese population from 17,000 to 27,000 between 1901 and 1911 and the number of Japanese from 4,750 to 9,000, public opinion was hostile and entries were effectively curbed by laying heavy taxes upon all Chinese arriving and by concluding an agreement with Japan whereby that country herself strictly limited departures for Canada.

Provincial government was established in Saskatchewan and Alberta in 1905.

Seven years later, a large portion of Northwest Territories was transferred to Manitoba. Clifford Sifton (1861-1929), Minister of the Interior from 1896 to 1911, was a dominating personality in this opening of the West.

Settlement was fostered by an unparalleled outburst of railroad construction. The Canadian Pacific, the first transcontinental line, built numerous branches running north and south in these years. Two other coast-to-coast systems, the Canadian Northern and the Grand Trunk Pacific, emerged between 1896-1906 and 1903-1916 respectively under the stimulus of land grants, cash subsidies, loans and guarantees. Superb transportation facilities resulted, but overbuilding and needless duplication led to a financial crisis early in the War.

Wheat was the great crop of the West. After 1909, the familiar Red Fife gave way to Marquis, an early-ripening variety developed by Dr. Charles Saunders (1867-). By 1914 Canada was one of the major wheat-producing areas of the world. The Hudson's Bay Railway, running across Manitoba to Fort Churchill, was designed to cut shipping distances to Liverpool nearly 1,000 miles. The first track was laid in 1911.

Agriculturalists in older sections found themselves unable to compete with wheat growers on the virgin lands of the West and now bent their energies in other directions. Dairying, fruit production and truck gardening became important industries in the Maritime Provinces, Quebec and Ontario. Fox farming developed into a leading occupation in Prince Edward Island which, however, suffered a 10 per cent decline in population.

Mining brought fabulous wealth to Ontario, Yukon Territory and British Columbia as did lumbering to the Maritimes, Quebec and British Columbia. Each year witnessed the discovery of new beds of precious and industrial minerals in the Laurentian Plateau and Cordilleran area. The lands below Hudson Bay and Hudson Strait, transferred to Ontario and Quebec respectively in 1912, were exceptionally rich in minerals. By 1913 Canada led the world in cobalt and nickel extraction and stood well to the fore in gold, silver, copper and asbestos production. Ore output then reached $145,500,000. Canadian lumber gained a world market while wood pulp and pulp logs became leading exports to the United States. The Temiskaming and Northern Ontario Railway, built by the Province of Ontario between 1900-1905, served the "New North".

Settlement of the West led to rapid industrialization in southern Ontario and Quebec. This was largely financed by British and American capital, with the latter gaining steadily in importance. American branch plants abounded by 1914. Nineteen thousand factories representing an investment of $1,250,000,000 were in operation in Canada by 1911, 8,000 of them being located in Ontario and 6,500 in Quebec. Production then reached one and a quarter billion dollars. Manufactured goods formed a steadily-declining percentage of total imports after 1900.

Canadian commerce, too, underwent astonishing development in these years. Exports rose from $192,000,000 in 1900 to $479,000,000 in 1913-1914 and imports from $190,000,000 to $651,000,000. Construction of great Atlantic and Pacific fleets by the Canadian Pacific Railway Company linked Canada to Great Britain and Australasia. American trade, however, made steady progress at the expense of the motherland and the Empire. Imports from the United Kingdom fell from 24.4

per cent of the total to 21.4 per cent between 1906 and 1914 and Empire imports from 29.5 per cent to 25 per cent while imports from the United States rose from 59.6 per cent to 64. Exports followed the same trend. American gains occurred despite tariff preference (one-third reduction after 1900) in favor of British goods and led to widespread demand for reciprocity with the United States.

The Liberal Party, led by Wilfrid Laurier (1841-1919), was in power from 1896-1911. Canadian contingents supported Great Britain in the Boer War. A sharp controversy respecting the Alaskan boundary was settled in America's favor by arbitration in 1903. Laurier's downfall arose through his advocacy of American reciprocity which won rural support but aroused powerful industrial and transportation interests and patriots who played on annexation fears. The Conservatives under Robert Borden (1854-   ) consequently triumphed at the polls in 1911. Their victory marked the full dawn of Canadian nationalism. Formation of a Canadian navy was announced the same year.

NEWFOUNDLAND

The years 1900-1914 formed a critical period in the history of this ancient dependency. The Dominion failed to recover from the panic of 1895. Canada's refusal to assume Newfoundland's debts and to admit it into the Confederation threw the islanders onto their own resources. Reconstruction proved most difficult. Fluctuations in the price of fish, Newfoundland's staple, and the growth of competitive whaling in the South Atlantic and of sealing in the North Pacific filled these years with grave uncertainty. However, the opening of pulp mills in 1909 and the discovery of new mineral deposits gave hope for the future. Robert Bond (1857-1927), premier from 1900 to 1909 and an ardent nationalist, advocated Newfoundland's solution of its own problems. A reciprocity treaty aimed at developing the island's resources was negotiated with the United States but unhappily failed in the American Senate. Old-age pensions were inaugurated in 1906. Rapid growth of the Fishermen's Protective Union, a cooperative productive and distributive society, did much to alleviate distress. Five branch railroads were projected in 1910 to facilitate marketing.

The Dominion figured in two international settlements of this period. Under the Entente Cordiale of 1904, France renounced her exclusive fishing rights off the western shore. A Hague Tribunal award in 1910 secured Great Britain's right to regulate Newfoundland fisheries without securing the United States' consent. A bitter conflict with Canada over title to Labrador, whose wood pulp resources gave it great value, opened in 1903. Newfoundland's claims were ultimately upheld by the British Privy Council in 1927.

The Dominion's trade rose from $16,600,000 in 1901 to $31,000,000 in 1913-1914. Commerce with Great Britain, the British Empire and the United States stood at $7,000,000, $7,700,000 and $7,475,000 respectively in the latter year.

BERMUDA AND THE CARIBBEAN COLONIES

From the turn of the century, Bermuda and the larger Caribbean colonies fell increasingly within the American orbit. The lesser islands, on the contrary, continued closely bound to the mother country. Bermuda developed into a favorite American playground and the United States became the primary market for its leading products, vegetables and lilies. In 1914 exports to the United States stood at £85,000 as against £5,200 to the United Kingdom while imports from the two totalled £350,000 and £135,000 respectively.

Sisal and fruit cultivation expanded rapidly in the Bahamas under American demand. By 1914 trade with the parent state was but £115,000 as against £378,000 with the United States. Jamaican banana production was stimulated by the appearance of the United Fruit Company as a heavy buyer. Trade with the United States in 1914 was £3,000,000—double that with Great Britain. Trinidad asphalt was shipped almost exclusively to the U. S. A. Trinidad's American commerce exceeded her British trade by £400,000 in 1914. Barbadian exports to the United States in 1914 (£75,000) were nearly double those to the United Kingdom.

This economic drift towards the States occasioned grave apprehension. The recruiting of Jamaican blacks for work on the Panama Canal and the well-intentioned landing of marines at Kingston after the destructive earthquake of 1907 likewise aroused considerable anti-American feeling. In 1909 a Royal Commission was named to study the question of closer relations between Canada and Britain's West India possessions. A reciprocal trade agreement, under which each gave the other a 20 per cent tariff preference, followed in 1912, and fortnightly steamer service subsidized by the Canadian Government opened shortly after.

Sugar cultivation, which had been dealt a staggering blow by the opening of the American market to shipments from the former Spanish colonies after 1898 and by the development of plantations in Hawaii following its annexation, rallied under the Brussels Convention of 1902 which abrogated bounties on European beet sugar. A sharp turn from monoculture nevertheless followed, with fruit and cacao as the preferred new crops. Banana acreage in Jamaica quadrupled between 1900 and 1914 while that in cacao rose 800 per cent. Population increase was general but Barbados, whose lands were exhausted, lost one-tenth of its inhabitants in the same years. The Institute of Jamaica, under the Secretaryship of Frank Cundall, now became a leading cultural center in the Empire.

Settlement of the Venezuelan boundary dispute in 1899 led to rapid expansion in British Guiana. Commerce rose from £3,500,000 in 1900-1901 to £5,400,000 in 1914. British Honduras likewise prospered. Its trade, however, was largely American—£794,000 in 1914 as against £166,000 with the motherland.

THE FALKLAND ISLANDS

The new century found these outposts of empire facing a dark future. The shift in trade lanes certain to follow the opening of the Panama Canal would destroy their importance as a coaling station. Sealing had virtually ended. Whaling was now restricted to South Georgia and had fallen into Norwegian hands. Sheep-farming, the only practical form of agricultural economy, met sharp competition from Australasia. The Argentine Republic had by no means abandoned its claims to the group. Rapid population increase (from 2,000 in 1901 to 3,200 in 1914) lessened economic opportunity. The naval station at Stanley, which had given employment to many, closed in 1904. An unhealthy social structure was likewise developing; whereas the ratio of males to females was three to two in 1901, the disproportion grew steadily and by 1914 it was three to one. On the eve of the War, the Falklands were generally regarded as a decadent possession and their further value to the motherland was a subject of common debate.

ASIA

INDIA

The turn of the twentieth century witnessed the inauguration of numerous reforms at the hands of the energetic new Viceroy, Lord Curzon (1859-1925), who had assumed office in 1899. The North West Frontier Province was organized and a radically different policy, coupling conciliation with firm control, was adopted towards the turbulent tribesmen along the Afghan border. Taxes were cut, the treasury was reorganized, a department of commerce and industry was created, the Empire's educational system and administrative machinery were thoroughly overhauled, the army was reconstructed and closer relations were established with the native princes. An expedition to Thibet brought the latter within the orbit of Indian affairs and averted the danger of Russian penetration. Government, however, continued exclusively in British hands—despite his rare gifts as an administrator, Curzon proved insensible to fresh currents of thought stirring the East and failed entirely to comprehend native aspirations. He resigned in 1905 following controversy with Lord Kitchener, Commander-in-Chief of the British army in India, over the latter's political status.

Militant nationalism emerged immediately after. European-educated Hindus, who had organized the Indian National Congress as the pioneer clearing-house for native opinion in 1885 and who had assembled in annual congresses for a generation, were now reinforced by Mohammedan patriots who founded the All-India Moslem League in 1906. Both bodies attained an importance wholly disproportionate to their unofficial character. The nationalist movement fattened on social discrimination and lack of economic opportunity for well-trained Indians and on widespread popular unrest rooted in the famines and plagues of the 90's. Nipponese victory in the Russo-Japanese War (1904-1905), shattering the myth of occidental invulnerability, and a doubling of the number of vernacular newspapers and magazines between 1900 and 1914 (there were 1,500 in the latter year), gave it powerful impetus.

The immediate incident precipitating conflict was the division of Bengal into two provinces. This step was taken in the interests of administrative efficiency shortly after the arrival of Lord Minto (1845-1914), Curzon's successor (r. 1905-1910). It gave great offense and led to a general boycott of British textiles (the "Swadeshi" movement) which degenerated into terrorism, and in 1909 an attempt was made on Minto's life.

Home authorities viewed the situation realistically. While meeting violence with a ruthless show of force, they sought to placate the Indians by granting them a direct voice in affairs. In 1907, John Morley (1838-1923), Secretary of State for India, named one Hindu and one Mohammedan Indian to his Council. The

"Morley-Minto Reforms", inaugurated by the Indian Councils Act, followed in 1909. Elected members were now added to both the central Legislative Council and the several provincial ones and official members ceased to form majorities in the latter. The legislatures, however, remained mere advisory bodies. Indians were likewise named to the Governor-General's Executive Council and corresponding bodies in the provinces. Two years later, on the occasion of the coronation durbar, the reconstitution of Bengal and the transfer of the capital from Calcutta to Delhi, ancient seat of Mogul glories, were announced. The Government now likewise undertook to protect Indian immigrants against disabilities in South Africa and Canada.

Such measures pacified moderates but stimulated extremists who now demanded "Swaraj"—home rule. In 1912, Lord Hardinge (1858-   ; r. 1910-1916), the Viceroy, narrowly escaped assassination on his state entry into Delhi. The eve of the War found the peninsula seething with disaffection.

The early twentieth century was a period of great prosperity. The population reached 247,000,000 by 1914, an increase of 16,000,000 since 1901. British residents rose from 96,500 to 125,000. With the spread of irrigation, the area under cultivation soared from 180 to 219 million acres, a quarter of this land being artificially watered. Cotton, jute, coffee and tea production mounted rapidly. Rural credit banks, established in 1904, fostered agricultural enterprise of all types. Industry likewise underwent remarkable expansion. Many textile mills appeared. The number of joint stock companies doubled, reaching 2,680 by 1914. Despite the boycott and a great famine in 1908, imports and exports both more than doubled between 1900 and 1914, standing at 2,350,000,000 and 2,560,000,000 rupees respectively in the latter year. Railroad trackage increased from 25,000 to 35,000 miles. India's economic importance within the Empire was never higher than in 1914 and its value to the mother country was incalculable.

CEYLON

The dawn of the new century found this fertile island in the last stages of a great agricultural revolution. Coffee, the staple product for almost a century, had been stricken by leaf disease about 1880. Recovery had proven impossible and tea had been introduced as a substitute crop. In 1900, but 17,500 acres were left in coffee as against 425,000 in tea. By 1914 coffee was no longer an export item while Ceylon had become a major tea producing area. A conspicuous figure in this transition was Sir Thomas Lipton (1850-1931) who popularized Singhalese tea throughout the world. Rubber cultivation, more recently become the dominant industry, was already well under way by 1900. Unlike tea production, it was largely in native hands. Tea exports in 1914 reached £6,000,000 and rubber exports £4,000,000. So rapid was agricultural extension that exports more than doubled in value between 1900 and the eve of the war (£15,650,000 in 1913.) An adverse trade balance of long standing was thus at length overcome.

Ceylon's population rose from 3,575,000 in 1900 to 4,250,000 in 1914. This swelled the rural proletariat and aggravated the social problem as the soil was largely in wealthy native and absentee British hands. Political unrest, likewise, appeared about 1905. Prosperous middle caste groups now demanded representation in the

Legislative Council and marked racial animosity developed. Moderate concessions made in 1909 added fuel to the flame and by 1914 the situation was tense.

MALAYA

Our period was one of rapid expansion and intense economic activity throughout this area. Christmas Island and the Cocos group were annexed to Straits Settlements early in the century and Labuan was merged with it in 1907. A Federal Council, with power to legislate for the Federated Malay States as a unit, was created in 1909 and knit the member states closely together. Protectorates were established over Kedah, Trengganu, Kelantan and Perlis the same year. In 1914 the Sultan of Johore, long the only state outside the federation, accepted a British adviser. Thus, on the outbreak of war, the British were in firm control throughout the lower half of the peninsula.

Straits Settlements, in particular, enjoyed a veritable boom. With the development of the canned food industry, tin mining flourished. Exports rose from six to nearly ten million pounds between 1900 and 1914. Rubber plantations, today found on every hand, were laid out under the impetus of demand from electrical and automobile manufacturers and began to yield about 1910. The colony's trade almost doubled (£102,000,000 in 1913) and Singapore, with its free port facilities, now became the commercial center of the Orient. The labor problem was solved by immigration, 240,000 Chinese and 120,000 Indians arriving in 1913 alone. Retail commerce fell increasingly into Chinese hands and by 1914 such competition was seriously affecting resident British traders.

Extensive railroad construction now opened up the Federated Malay States. Chinese settlers and capital poured in, tin mining and rubber planting became leading industries and the several countries underwent rapid economic transformation. By 1914 identical trends were discernable in the unfederated section, Johore.

The development of North Borneo, Brunei and Sarawak was less spectacular. Here too, however, there was marked progress. The British North Borneo Company's rule was extended over Tembunan following the death of Muhammad Saleh, the last independent native leader, during a military campaign in 1900. In 1904, Rajah Charles Johnson Brooke (1829-1917; r. 1868-1917) of Sarawak acquired additional lands from the North Borneo Company in exchange for coal mining rights. Two years later, the Sultan of Brunei yielded his administrative functions to a British resident. All these territories fell increasingly under Singapore's commercial sway. A railroad completed in 1902 opened the interior of North Borneo and tobacco cultivation rapidly spread. Trade consequently doubled between 1900 and 1914, reaching £1,285,000 in the latter year. British demand caused sago production to attain considerable importance in Brunei. Rajah Brooke's capable rule and his sedulous protection of native interests led to the universal recognition of Sarawak as a model exploitation area. Its immense resources had, however, barely been tapped by 1914.

THE ENCLAVES
Aden

With the development of India and the rapid growth of Britain's Asiatic trade, Aden became a leading coaling station in the early years of the new century. Considerable hinterland was acquired through two Anglo-Turkish conventions of 1905 and 1914. Both transshipments and commerce with the interior of Arabia grew and trade rose from £4,500,000 in 1900 to £6,000,000 in 1914. Aden coffee now became a familiar item on the world market. A project to detach the region from Bombay Presidency and to convert it into a separate Crown Colony failed to materialize and it continued to be administered from India.

Hong Kong

The port of Cowloon and Lan-tao Island (the "New Territories"), acquired from China under 99-year lease in 1898, were occupied and attached to Hong Kong Crown Colony in 1899. The latter thus attained an area of 391 sq. m., eleven times its former size, while its population rose from 200,000 to 300,000. Cotton mills were opened and spinning and weaving had become important industries by 1914. With improved free port facilities and the opening of the Hong Kong-Canton Railway in 1910, trade developed rapidly and exceeded £6,000,000 annually by 1914. A heavy influx of Chinese raised the population to 460,000 by that year and raised many social problems which brought on considerable unrest. Racial feeling was, however, markedly absent.

Weihaiwei

Weihaiwei, along the Yellow Sea, was leased from China in 1898. Plans to fortify it were laid aside at the close of the Boxer War and it became a flying navy base. An exceptionally salubrious climate made it a favorite summer resort for westerners resident in the Far East. Rule by a civilian commissioner was instituted in 1901. Free port status led to marked commercial expansion which brought prosperity to the entire community. By 1914 the British were deeply entrenched.

THE INDIAN OCEAN ISLANDS

Increasing world demand for tropical commodities gave these possessions new significance. Copra production on a large scale was undertaken in the Andamans, the Nicobars and the Laccadives, dependencies of India, and in the Maldive group, attached to Ceylon. Monthly freight service to the Seychelles opened in 1901 and coconut oil and vanilla exports mounted rapidly thereafter. Extensive rubber plantations were laid out there about 1910. Sugar exports from Mauritius soared from £2,500,000 in 1900 to £3,850,000 in 1914. This colony was now completely inundated by Indian immigrants. In 1911, they numbered 258,000 out of a total population of 377,000. Business establishments and plantations alike passed rapidly into their hands—by 1914, Europeans had been largely dispossessed. Under the circumstances, an increase of elected seats in the Legislative Council between 1901 and 1913, virtually converting it into a representative body, occasioned considerable alarm among old-time families. However, no untoward incidents developed and these constitutional reforms did much to stabilize insular society.

AUSTRALASIA

THE COMMONWEALTH OF AUSTRALIA

The Australian Commonwealth came into being on January 1, 1901 through the voluntary entry of Queensland, New South Wales, Victoria, South Australia, Western Australia and Tasmania into a federal union. The American rather than the Canadian pattern was followed in creating the new Dominion. Only stated powers were assigned the central Government while residual ones continued vested in the several states. There were, however, two important differences between the American and Australian structures. In the Commonwealth, representative government was combined with responsible government and constitutional amendment was relatively easy. The constitution nevertheless proved surprisingly rigid. Only one amendment, increasing the central Government's responsibility by authorizing the assumption of state debts incurred after union, was adopted before 1914, while nine others, seeking to strengthen its position by augmenting its revenues and extending its authority, were rejected. Melbourne served as the provisional seat of government and the first Parliament assembled in May 1901. In 1908 the Canberra region in New South Wales was selected as a federal district. Plans for a capital city, submitted in open competition by Walter Griffin of Chicago, were accepted in 1913, and the foundation stones of Canberra were laid the same year.

Labor dominated political life in both the states and the central Government between 1901 and 1914. All industry was subjected to the control of special state boards empowered to regulate wages and arbitrate disputes. A federal arbitration act adopted in 1904 facilitated the settlement of industrial conflicts extending beyond a single state. The Labor Party, in general, held the balance of power to 1908. Thereafter, it was normally in control with Andrew Fisher (1862-1928) as Premier. Old age pensions were instituted in 1908 and maternity bonuses in 1912. Protection and the "White Australia" policy both took firm root in 1914. The transfer of Papua from Queensland and of Northern Territory from South Australia to the Commonwealth in 1906 and 1911 respectively and the assumption of control over surplus revenues in 1908 materially increased the central Government's independence and dignity. Australian bank notes appeared in 1910 and the Commonwealth Bank opened in 1913.

Defense was viewed as a Commonwealth problem from the outset. An Australian navy was created in 1909 and compulsory military training was inaugurated two years later. Thus by 1914 the trend towards centralization was clearly discernable and states' rights philosophy was already on the defensive.

Mining reached its greatest heights in this period. Maximum gold extraction was attained in 1903, tin yield in 1907 and silver-lead output in 1913. With the exhaustion of deposits in the three eastern states, Western and South Australia became leading producers and underwent rapid development. A bounty act of 1914 fostered the Dominion's iron industry.

Ranching and agriculture gained steadily in importance. A great drought in 1902 brought only a temporary setback. Wheat production reached 25,000,000 bu. by 1914-1915; wool exports, £22,000,000; and meat exports £10,000,000 as against gold exports of only £2,700,000.

Industry, too, made vast strides. Thanks to the stimulus afforded by protection, there were 15,500 factories in operation by 1913. They employed one-fifth of all workers and their output totalled £61,500,000 as against £107,000,000 from pastoral pursuits and farming and £26,000,000 from mining. Construction of a transcontinental railway widened the marketing area and opened the interior to exploitation. While population rose from 3,750,000 in 1901 to nearly 5,000,000 in 1915, Australia continued the most sparsely populated continent. The increase noted was largely through birth. Immigration was discouraged in an effort to maintain a high standard of living. South Europeans, and Italians in particular, with their tendency to undermine local labor markets, were systematically excluded. The inhabitants therefore continued almost exclusively of British stock. Trade with Great Britain stood at £82,500,000 in 1913 and that with Germany and America, the metropole's nearest rivals, about £12,000,000 each.

NEW ZEALAND

The great depression of the 90's was followed by a period of unbroken prosperity lasting until after the close of the First World War. Farming continued the paramount industry. Grain production, however, steadily gave way to ranching and dairying. Cereal acreage declined 12 per cent between 1900 and 1913 and wheat output from 6,500,000 bushels to 5,180,000. Wool exports, on the other hand, rose from 140,700,000 lbs. to 220,500,000; frozen meat exports from 1,850,000 cwt. to 3,230,000; butter exports from 172,500 cwt. to 435,000; and cheese exports from 103,000 cwt. to 864,000. Cooperatives flourished among dairymen and by 1914 dominated the industry. A Board of Agriculture was established in 1913. Gold output reached 500,000 oz. in 1909 and then steadily declined. Silver production quintupled between 1900 and 1909 but sank rapidly thereafter. Because of capital's fear of state socialism, manufacturing continued relatively undeveloped through the first decade of the century. Such fear was, however, ultimately dispelled and, with the growth of white population (from 700,000 in 1896 to 1,000,000 in 1911) and of national consciousness, rapid expansion followed. Growth in the textile and metallurgical industries was particularly notable.

In 1901, the home Government attached Rarotonga, Aitutaki, Niue and Penrhyn to New Zealand as dependencies. Six years later, this thriving colony was accorded Dominion status. Immigrants rose from 18,000 in 1900 to 44,500 in 1913. With Asiatics rigidly excluded and numerous restrictions limiting entries from southern Europe, the vast majority were of British stock and New Zealand continued more nearly purely British than any other portion of the Empire.

The Progressive Party, which had gained control in 1891, continued in power until 1912. Under the leadership of Richard Seddon (d. 1906) and his successor, Joseph Ward, New Zealand now became the world's foremost laboratory in social experimentation. Workman's compensation was introduced in 1900 and state fire insurance in 1903. Old age pensions (1898) were greatly extended in 1905 and 1913. Public housing was inaugurated in 1905. Industrial arbitration (1895) became firmly established through measures adopted in 1901 and 1908 which strengthened the system. The second ballot, for use when no candidate secured a majority vote, was established in 1908. A graduated land tax likewise broke up great estates. Government expenditures for education trebled between 1900 and 1913, reaching £1,335,000 in the latter year. Water power was made a state monopoly in 1908 and government hydro-electric installations followed at a rapid rate. However, the old Conservatives, now constituting the Reform Party, regained control in 1912 under William Massey (1856-1925) and stemmed the tide by abolishing perpetual state ownership of unalienated land (1892) and reintroducing freehold sale (1913). The eve of the War was darkened by violent strikes led by the new Labor Party, organized in 1910.

Six hundred seventy-five miles of state railways were built in our period, making a total of some 3,000. By 1914 but 29 miles remained in private hands. Imports rose from £10,650,000 in 1900 to £22,300,000 in 1913 and exports from £13,250,000 to £23,000,000. As always, trade was carried on chiefly with the United Kingdom, Australia and the United States. Most striking was the development of Canadian trade which, in 1913, exceeded £1,000,000.

The early years of the century witnessed a rapid spread of interest in Maori civilization and a vogue for native art which safeguarded it from extinction.

New Zealand infantrymen participated in the Boer War. The Defense Act of 1909 inaugurated compulsory military training and the Naval Defense Act of 1913 established a sea force on the basis of voluntary enlistments. The annual contribution toward the cost of British naval defense was increased from £20,000 to £40,000 in 1903 and to £100,000 in 1908. The cruiser *New Zealand* was likewise presented to the home Government.

OCEANIA

TERRITORIAL READJUSTMENTS

The acrimonious Samoan Islands controversy which had threatened war between Great Britain, Germany and the United States in 1889 was at length amicably settled at the turn of the century. By treaty of 1899, the British withdrew from the Samoan archipelago and received a portion of the German Solomons as compensation. The Entente Cordiale of 1904 provided for a settlement of Anglo-French claims in the New Hebrides and condominium rule followed in 1906. Meanwhile, a protectorate was at length established over the Tonga Islands (1900) which had long been within the United Kingdom's orbit and Ocean Island, annexed in 1901, became the administrative center of the Gilbert and Ellice group.

ECONOMIC DEVELOPMENT

Insatiable demand for hot-clime products led to the opening of periodic steamer service between Britain's scattered Pacific possessions and to rapid agricultural expansion there. Advance was especially marked in the Fijis. 23,000 Indians entered in the single decade 1901-1911 to man the new plantations and by 1913 formed a third of the entire population. Coconut acreage doubled between 1900 and 1914 while that in bananas and sugar cane trebled and rubber cultivation was introduced on a large scale. The trade of Fiji virtually trebled in the same period (£2,320,000 in 1914). The Tongas, the Gilbert and Ellice Islands and the British Solomons all made notable progress—only the New Hebrides, whose joint ownership by Britain and France discouraged investment, lagged behind. A notable feature of such development was the growth of commerce with Australia, Canada and non-British lands, particularly Germany and the United States.

THE MEDITERRANEAN "LIFE-LINE"

The rapid economic growth of India, Malaya, Australia, New Zealand and Oceania and the tremendous expansion of Britain's Asiatic and Pacific trade gave added significance to the Mediterranean holdings protecting her line of communication with the Orient.

A deep harbor affording anchorage for the entire fleet in those waters and a new dockyard were constructed at Gibraltar. Malta now gave way to the latter as a naval station of primary importance but, with the growth of British Far Eastern commerce, it became a leading port of call and enjoyed great prosperity. To meet growing demand for self-government, representative elements were introduced in the Executive Council in 1909. Political discontent was especially marked among Italian residents. No serious complications had, however, arisen by 1914.

Harbor facilities in Cyprus were improved but the island remained primarily agricultural. Irrigation works extended cultivation appreciably and trade rose from £625,000 in 1900 to nearly £1,250,000 by the eve of conflict. French and Greek interests grew far more rapidly than Great Britain's. An abrogation of Turkish sovereignty would inevitably bring clashing interests to the fore and give birth to grave complications.

GREAT BRITAIN

The close of the nineteenth century found British imperialism riding at full tide. Within a single generation, much of Africa, Asia and the Pacific Basin had been brought within the Empire while earlier acquisitions such as Canada, Australia and New Zealand were fast attaining their majority. Commerce and industry had reached unprecedented heights. Wages and living standards were steadily rising; prosperity was widespread. Great Britain was the richest, most powerful nation on earth and it was commonly held that her colonies had made her so.

The pageantry attending Victoria's Diamond Jubilee (1897) fired even the most stolid citizen. Pride in empire was universal. Britain's assumption of "The White Man's Burden" attained religious complexion in the popular mind. The reconquest of the Soudan and French humiliation in the Fashoda Crisis when France was obliged to lay aside her plans for a vast trans-African empire were hailed as evidences of divine favor. Rudyard Kipling (1865-1936), the personification of imperialism, was the most widely-read author of the day and Rhodes, South Africa's great empire builder, was a national hero. Imperial sentiment likewise gripped Britain's far-flung possessions. The 2-cent Canadian postage stamp of 1898—a world map in Mercator projection with British territories in bold carmine, inscribed "We hold a vaster empire than has been"—symbolized the new age.

The South African War provided a rude jolt. The Boers' stubborn refusal to accept the manifold blessings of the imperial connection was matched by world-wide condemnation of Britain's aggression and denunciation of her methods. The naval race with Germany, the latter's inroads on British commerce and the alignment of continental powers into two armed camps placed the British in a difficult position and destroyed the last vestiges of their old complacency. Two solutions were ultimately evolved: effecting understandings with two traditional rivals, France and Russia, and tightening the bonds of empire, a matter of primary concern to us here.

The colonial conference now became an established institution. It was agreed in 1902, at a gathering marking Edward VII's accession, to convene periodically thenceforth and meetings were held in 1907 and 1911. In 1907, in recognition of the dominions' increased importance, the title "Imperial Conference" was adopted. The British Prime Minister rather than the Colonial Secretary now presided and a permanent organization was effected. The creation of an Imperial General Staff was recommended and close cooperation between the dominions and the Imperial Defense Committee followed. In 1911 dominion statesmen were taken into full confidence in the matter of foreign affairs. New Zealand urged the creation of an Imperial Council of State and Court of Appeal. Shortly after, the home Government proposed that the dominions station ministers in London. These steps had not, however, been taken by the outbreak of war.

Joseph Chamberlain (1836-1914), Secretary of State for the Colonies from 1895 to 1903, likewise sought to integrate the Empire economically. He urged the abandonment of free trade in the face of mounting tariff barriers abroad and advocated converting all British lands into a single unit against the outer world by a system of preferential duties. While protecting colonial industry against competition from the metropole, such arrangements would foster intra-Empire relations and strengthen imperial ties. But protection was, as yet, too much at variance with British tradition. Disruption of the Unionist Party and Chamberlain's resignation followed. The project was dropped after a smashing Liberal victory in 1906 and the experiment was consequently not undertaken until after the World War. But homeland sentiment fostered a powerful "Buy Empire" movement which met notable response overseas. Canada had granted preferential rates on British goods in 1897. Cape Colony followed suit in 1903 and New Zealand in 1907. British trade with British lands thus rose from an annual average of £198,000,000 between 1894 and 1903 to an annual average of £306,000,000 in the decade 1904-1913.

Imperial consciousness evinced itself in other ways. Empire penny postage was launched in 1898. Rhodes Scholarships were established for every important British possession. The Imperial Institute at South Kensington, devoted to a study of economic problems throughout the Empire, was accorded official status in 1907. Whereas, in 1900, but one-third of Great Britain's emigrants settled within her outlying possessions, by 1913 four-fifths did so. Thus, as political ties weakened, economic and cultural bonds were strengthened. Britain's position throughout the world had never been stronger than in 1914.

Chapter III

The French Empire
AFRICA

FRENCH NORTH AFRICA (MAGHREB)

Algeria

THE opening of the twentieth century witnessed a determined effort on the part of the French to subjugate the upper reaches of the Sahara lying south of Algeria. The latter had been conquered between 1830-1848, had been made an integral part of France in 1871[1] and was well-developed by 1900. Further expansion was now deemed desirable to safeguard the settled area against nomadic attack and to link Algeria and Tunis with French West and Equatorial Africa which were rapidly taking shape. The Insala Oasis was occupied in December 1899, the Tuat Oases in 1900 and Colomb Bechar, adjoining the Moroccan boundary, in 1903. Despite reverses, the region was speedily pacified by Governor Jonnart (r. 1900-1901 and 1903-1911) and General Lyautey (1854-1934). Construction of a railroad to Colomb Bechar (1905) facilitated matters and by 1906 native resistance was broken. Meanwhile, in 1902, these Saharan lands, ten times the extent of Algeria proper, were organized as Southern Territories.

The old policy of centralization and assimilation was replaced in 1898 by decentralization and adaptation of French institutions to local conditions. Financial delegations, representing both French colonists and natives, were created to discuss imposts and when, in 1900, a separate Algerian budget was established, these bodies and the Superior Council were empowered to vote it. The French Parliament, in which Algeria enjoyed representation[2], continued to legislate for the country.

The population rose from 4.7 to 5.7 million between 1901 and 1914. The gulf between the natives (4.9 million in 1914) and European residents (800,000, of whom but 500,000 were French) was increasingly narrowed by legislation. A law of 1897, governing the division of tribal lands, created a large body of petty proprietors by the eve of the War. Natives were regularly conscripted after 1912. A homesteading law of 1904 brought in considerable numbers of Spanish settlers. By 1914 a large proportion of the Europeans were Algerian-born (commonly half French,

---

[1] The country was divided into three departments and was, of course, under the control of the French Parliament like any portion of France proper, rather than of the Ministry of Colonies.
[2] Six seats in the Chamber of Deputies (2 per department) and three in the Senate (1 per department).

The Fren

30	60	90	120	150	180	

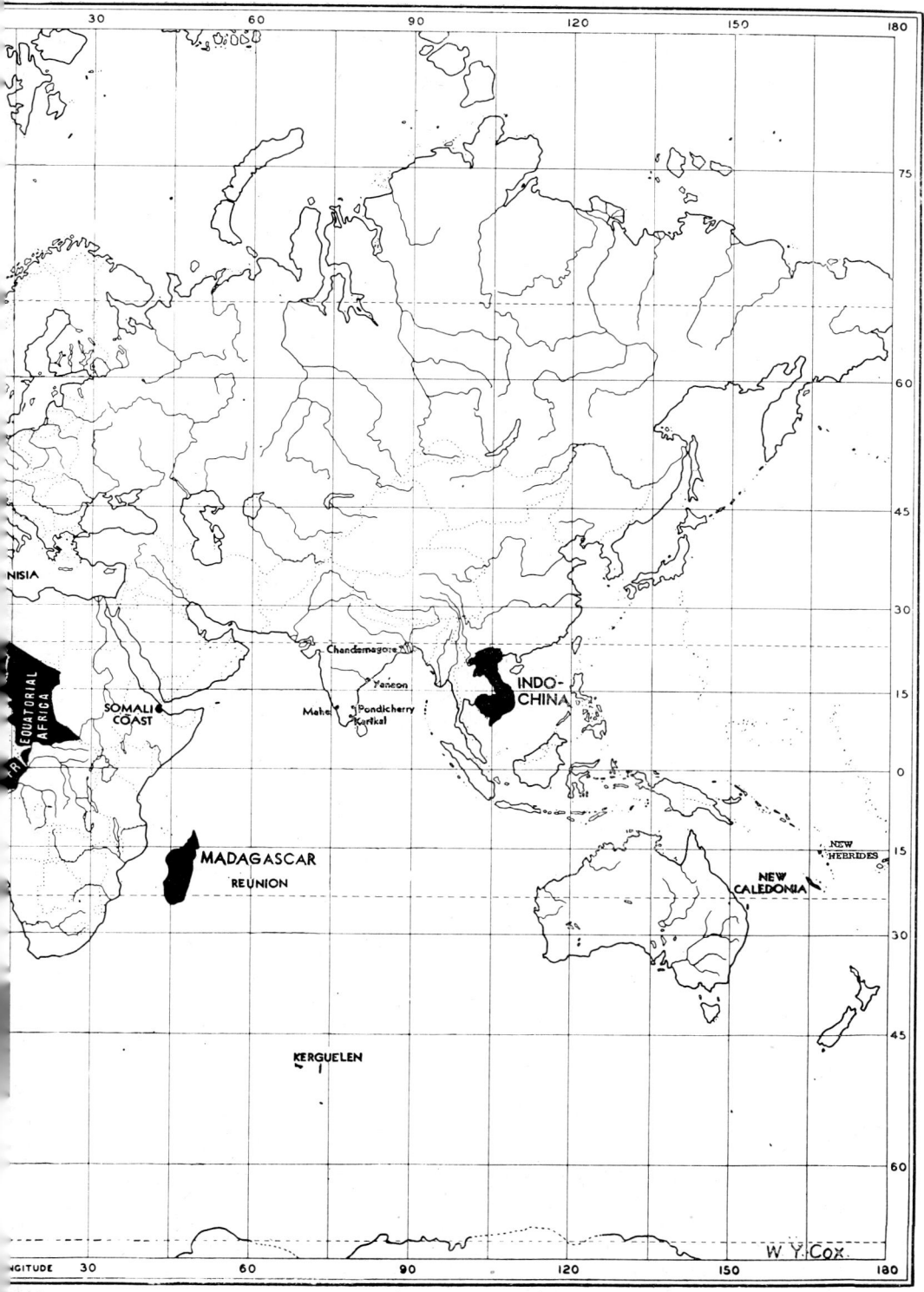

NISIA

SOMALI COAST

EQUATORIAL AFRICA

Chandernagore
Yanaon
Mahe
Pondicherry
Karikal

INDO-CHINA

MADAGASCAR
REUNION

NEW HEBRIDES

NEW CALEDONIA

KERGUELEN I

W. Y. Cox

1914

half Spanish) and strong local sentiment had emerged. There was, however, no agitation for independence.

Viniculture, sericulture and olive and wheat production enjoyed steady progress. Wine output rose from 145 million gallons in 1900 to 227 million in 1914. Cotton planting was undertaken in 1906 with a fair degree of success. Mines nearly quadrupled in number in the same period and iron, lead and phosphate extraction soared. Rapid railroad construction, raising trackage from 1,800 to 2,800 miles, led to marked development in outlying regions. Both exports and imports doubled between 1900 and 1913, reaching 510 and 667 million francs respectively in the latter year. Nearly three-fourth's of Algeria's total external trade was then carried on with the metropole—France's commerce with this prosperous African community virtually equalled that with all her other possessions combined. Pre-war Algeria thus effectively refuted the common charge that, despite their long experience, the French had not yet mastered the art of colonization.

Tunis

Turkish assent to a delimitation of the Tunisian-Tripolitanian frontier was won in 1910 after protracted negotiations, but the Ottoman Empire steadfastly refused to recognize the establishment of a French protectorate over Tunis in the 80's and had not yet done so by 1914. This, however, posed no serious difficulty since, with Italy's reluctant acceptance of an accomplished fact in 1896, effective opposition had ceased.

The European population grew rapidly in the new century. The French element showed the greatest rate of increase, doubling between 1900 and 1913 (50,000 in the latter year). There were, however, 110,000 Italians in the Regency by 1913 and they then embraced considerably more than half the aliens. The Anglo-Maltese, on the contrary, remained stationary at 13,000. Such over-preponderance of Italians raised serious questions. Although the preservation of their nationality was guaranteed under the convention of 1896 which likewise permitted the Italian Government to operate schools for their benefit, consistent efforts were made to Gallicize them. These were stoutly resisted and occasioned much bad blood between the two immigrant groups. Economic problems added to the strain. In 1912 the Italians held but 210,000 acres of land against 1,790,000 in French hands and feeling on the score rode high.

The native population showed little change (1,800,000 on the outbreak of war). Political unrest appeared among young, western-educated Tunisians early in the century and, as the rising generation which had not known the iniquities of the old regime came to the fore, opposition to the protectorate became marked. In 1902 the railways were placed under Tunisian control. Natives were admitted to the Resident General's Consultative Conference five years later. Law codification was effected in 1914 when provision was likewise made for converting tribal lands into private holdings. Far from allaying discontent, these measures served to fire nationalist hopes. Fortunately, however, Sidi Mohamed, who ascended the throne in 1906, proved loyal to the French connection and no disorders had occurred by 1914.

Agriculture continued the basic industry, with cereals, olives, dates and wine as the chief products. Scientific methods adopted by the Europeans greatly increased production but native output continued low. Viniculture (44,000 acres in 1913, yielding 6 million gallons of wine) was almost exclusively European. The number of mines in operation trebled in 15 years, reaching 32 in 1913. Iron extraction first attained importance in this period (600,000 tons in 1913). Lead and zinc production grew steadily. Tunis now likewise became a leading source of supply for phosphate, production rising from 150,000 tons in 1900 to 2,100,000 in 1913. A trebling of railroad trackage was largely connected with such exploitation of the country's mineral resources.

Commerce rose from 104 million francs in 1900 to 325 million in 1913. Owing to high protective tariffs adopted in 1897 with privileged treatment accorded French wares in Tunis and Tunisian wines in France and to the creation of a Franco-Tunisian-Algerian customs union for cereals, nearly half of the Regency's commerce fell to France. Trade with Italy reached less than a fourth as much—but 35 million francs in 1913. Close relations with France were fostered by the coordination of the Algerian and Tunisian railways, by the opening of a new port at Bizerte and by the Bank of Algeria which extended its operations to Tunis shortly before the War.

The Industrial Revolution had not yet, in 1914, reached the Regency. For example, ore was shipped out for reduction elsewhere. Even Tunisian wheat was milled in Marseilles.

Morocco

The Sherifian Empire was the choicest portion of Africa still free from European control at the turn of the new century. Its resources and commercial potentialities were great and its geographic position gave it enormous strategic value. Anglo-British-Spanish rivalry had preserved its independence but foreign influence was already much in evidence. The Sultan's army was headed by British, French, German, Italian and Spanish officers and his fleet was commanded by Germans. The British, French and German Governments operated their own postoffices in the country. France minted Morocco's coins. Nearly half its foreign trade (35 out of 85 million francs) was in British hands. French investments exceeded 25 million francs. The ports swarmed with concession hunters. Now, as an aftermath of humiliations attending the Fashoda Crisis, Théophile Delcassé (1852-1923), French Minister of Foreign Affairs from 1898 to 1905, undertook to bring the country within France's orbit.

Franco-Italian understandings of 1900 and 1902 gave France free rein in Morocco in return for according Italy an unrestrained hand in Tripoli-Cyrenaica. Great Britain's consent was won by accepting her occupation of Egypt under the Entente Cordiale agreement of 1904. A convention with Spain, dividing Morocco into two spheres of influence (1904), bought off that country.

Conditions were meanwhile shaping themselves so as to bring on intervention. The Sultan's authority had declined greatly during Abdul-Aziz' (b. 1878; r. 1894-1908) minority and the country lay in chaos. The monarch was a gullible youth who readily fell victim to adventurers and emptied the treasury through gross personal extravagance. A loan floated in Paris in 1904 on outrageous terms with the Moroccan customs revenue as security was but the first of several ultimately totalling 334 million francs. French occupation of the Moroccan-Algerian hinterland began in 1899. An understanding whereby the French undertook to police the Moroccan-Algerian frontier was negotiated and the construction of a strategic railway through western Algeria followed.

But all calculations were upset when, on March 31, 1905, William II made a dramatic landing at Tangier, hailed Abdul-Aziz as an independent sovereign and announced Germany's intention of protecting her nationals' interests in the Sultanate against French encroachment. The episode led to Delcassé's retirement and prevented the immediate establishment of a protectorate.

Halting progress was, however, made. While the Algeciras Conference of 1906 reaffirmed Morocco's independence, France was accorded a privileged position in the internationalized State Bank, and Spain and she were authorized to police the seaports. In actual practice, each was soon supreme in its own sphere as delimited in 1904. Casablanca was occupied by France in 1907 following native disorders. A year later, Abdul-Aziz, whose Francophobism occasioned grave concern, was deposed by a more tractable brother, Mulai Hafid, who was accorded Gallic support. The latter promptly accepted a Paris loan and summoned the French to his rescue in 1911 when a formidable rebellion imperilled his position. Meanwhile, in 1909, Germany recognized France's political interests upon that country's accepting an economic condominium, and numerous Franco-German syndicates for exploiting the Sultanate sprang into being.

France's occupation of Fez while reestablishing Mulai Hafid led to the dispatch of the German gunboat *Panther* to Agadir. Though not opposed to the establishment of a protectorate, Germany sought compensation such as had already been accorded Italy, Great Britain and Spain. A transaction whereby France ceded to Germany portions of French Equatorial Africa giving Kamerun outlets through the Congo and Ubangi basins was concluded on November 4, 1911 and the protectorate was at length proclaimed on March 30, 1912. In November, Spanish Morocco, envisaged by the Franco-Spanish Convention of 1904, was established.

These events precipitated wide-spread insurrection. Lyautey, fresh from his Algerian triumph, was named Resident-General and acted with despatch. Mulai Hafid was pensioned off and his brother, Mulai Yusef, who proved more acceptable to the chieftains, was proclaimed Sultan in August 1912. The country was then methodically occupied district by district and was firmly under French control by July 1914.

Lyautey displayed consummate skill in conciliating the tribesmen. Local institutions were left intact. Roads, markets, hospitals and schools were opened on a lavish scale. Indeed, so successful was he in demonstrating the value of the French connection that little difficulty was experienced in maintaining order in the new protectorate on the outbreak of war.

Agriculture and industry were still primitive in 1914. Viniculture, cotton planting and factories had, however, already been introduced by the French. Extensive railway and harbor projects were likewise in progress. Morocco's foreign trade in 1913 stood at 326 million francs—four times its value in 1900. Half fell to France and Algeria. Great Britain's share, on the contrary, stood at a mere 60 million—far below the earlier figure. The success of the Moroccan venture was then already evident. It was, indeed, destined to be one of the most profitable in the annals of European expansion.

FRENCH WEST AFRICA ("A. O. F.")

Three Anglo-French agreements of 1898, 1899 and 1906 and a Franco-Spanish convention of 1900 cleared the way for France's occupation of the heart of West Africa. The Upper Niger basin, the central and western Soudan and the Sahara were all promptly annexed early in the twentieth century. Such expansion was stoutly opposed by the natives, most redoubtable of whom were the Saharan Tuareg. But the occupation of two oases strongholds, Air (1905) and Bilma (1906) in the east, and of the Adrar Temur region (1909) in the west, broke all resistance and, with the subjection of the Tibesti highland adjoining Italian Libya in 1916, French West Africa reached its present territorial limits.

The four old coastal colonies, Senegal, French Guinea, Ivory Coast and Dahomey, which had been grouped together in 1895 to form the Governor-Generalship of French West Africa, were now linked through extensive territorial additions in the hinterland. The military district of Zinder, between the Niger and Lake Chad, was created in 1900 and the military district of Mauritania, north of Senegal, in the years 1903-1909. A fifth colony, Upper Senegal-Niger, was formed in the interior in 1904. Liberia and British, German, Spanish and Portuguese holdings along the Atlantic coast bulge of West Africa thereafter formed enclaves in a vast French domain.

The systematic exploitation of agricultural and forest resources dates from the turn of the century. Haphazard production by the natives now gave way to large-scale plantation and silvicultural enterprises which enormously increased production. Ground nuts, rubber, timber, palm oil and cotton became the chief products of Senegal, Guinea, Ivory Coast, Dahomey and Upper Senegal-Niger respectively. The wild trees of French West Africa yielded one-ninth the world's supply of rubber in 1910.

The Bank of West Africa, founded in 1901, played an important role in developing the area. St. Louis, Dakar, Konakri, Grand Bassam and Kontonu became important shipping centers. Exports rose from 74 to 122 million francs between 1900-1913 and imports from 85 to 146 million. Much of this commerce was, however, in British and German hands.

Bad communication at first hindered the development of the interior. However the lease of two tracts along the Niger from Great Britain in 1903 and the latter's cession of Yarbatenda, a port on the Gambia, in 1904, provided important river outlets. Railroad construction was likewise begun in Guinea, Ivory Coast and Dahomey and the Senegalese system was extended into Upper Senegal-Niger. By 1914, 1,500 miles were in operation, linking the Niger and Senegal Rivers, traversing Senegal and leading into the interiors of the other coastal colonies. The inauguration of steamer service from Timbuktu to Koulikoro on the upper Niger, the eastern terminal of the Senegal-Niger railway, placed the heart of West Africa in direct touch with France on the eve of the First World War. Some 10,000 Europeans then resided in the Governor-Generalship and the region was viewed as a land of great potentialities. A trans-Saharan railroad, extending from Algeria to Timbuktu, was already under consideration.

The several colonies within French West Africa were developed as portions of a single great administrative district, a given one complementing the others in a variety of ways. Each had its separate executive and retained its administrative and financial autonomy. The central government, which served their common interests, was headed by a Governor-General and a Council sitting at Dakar.

Native relations were excellent. The policy of association was followed and local customs and institutions were generally respected. Only rulers such as the King of Abomey in Dahomey who proved openly hostile to the new regime were deposed. Medical service on a large scale was provided. The Arab slave traders' activities were likewise curbed. An appreciable population increase was, consequently, evident by 1914. There were then 12,500,000 natives within the area. Various expedients were employed to win African support. So far as possible, rulers' sons were induced to attend French schools. Temporary alliances with tribal women and the procreation of half-breeds were encouraged. The opening of markets proved economically advantageous to the blacks. Some 15,000 males admitted to military service gained great prestige thereby, provided France with an inexpensive army and afforded cheap insurance against local uprisings. By 1914 French military experts viewed West Africa as a huge reservoir of men from which millions of sturdy fighters might be drawn to augment the insufficient forces provided by the home country's stationary population. The World War was destined to bring this dream to realization.

FRENCH EQUATORIAL AFRICA ("A. E. F.")

Savorgnan de Brazza's (1852-1905) explorations north of the Congo and Ubangi Rivers, which had given birth to the French Congo, were continued at the close of the century by Emile Gentil (1866-   ) and Jean Marchand (1863-1934) who pushed farther east and north into the interior. Gentil's navigation of the Shari River and Lake Chad (1896-1897) and Marchand's notable feat of traversing the heart of Africa from the Ubangi to the upper Nile (1896-1898) gave France effective claim to the western Soudan if not to the White Nile valley, as had been hoped. The Anglo-French declaration of March 1899, terminating the Fashoda Crisis, cleared the way for France's occupation of the former area.

This was accomplished through the junction of three military expeditions on the shores of Lake Chad in April 1900—the Foureau-Lamy Mission which had crossed the Sahara from Algeria, the Central African Mission (headed first by Voulet and Chanoine, who fell victims to the climate and ran amock, and subsequently by Joalland and Meynier) and the Gentil Mission from French Congo. Combining forces, they broke the power of Rabah Zobeir, a half-breed Arab chieftain dominating the area, and his sons (1900-1901) and established firm control. The state of Kanem, lying east of Lake Chad, was conquered in 1902; Wadai, adjoining the Anglo-Egyptian Sudan, between 1903 and 1912; and Borku, south of Libya, in 1913. These lands east of Lake Chad were subsequently explored by Jean Tilho between 1912 and 1917.

In 1904 the area was organized into the military district of Chad and three colonies, Gabon, Middle Congo and Ubangi-Shari, with Gentil as Commissioner-General. The collective name of French Equatorial Africa was adopted six years later. Its unity was broken in 1911 when Germany gained two portions of Middle Congo in return for according France a free hand in Morocco but allied victory in the World War led to its ultimate reconstruction.

Economic development was slow. Poor transportation was, in part, responsible. While Gabon fronted the Atlantic, the Congo rapids cut Middle Congo and Ubangi-Shari off from the sea. A railroad connecting Brazzaville in Middle Congo with the port of Loango in Gabon was projected but failed to materialize. These two colonies' only outlets in 1914 were consequently by road across Gabon or by rail from Stanley Pool through the Belgian Congo. The privilege of free commercial access to the Nile, enjoyed under the Anglo-French declaration of 1899, proved of little practical value and Chad lay almost untouched.

The natives were likewise few in number, of inferior stock and suffering progressive decimation through sleeping sickness and leprosy. Numerous European ailments introduced by the whites, alcoholism following in the latter's wake and the destruction of livestock through the spread of the tsetse fly added to the general horror and desolation. The population declined from twelve million in 1900 to nine million in 1913. Settlers were few (there were but 700 Frenchmen in Gabon as late as 1913) and small investors fought shy of the area. Concessions were consequently granted on a lavish scale.

Enormous areas bestowed upon some forty corporations at the turn of the century were exploited as trading monopolies. One grant alone was one-fifth the size of France. Periodic deliveries of produce were demanded by way of taxes and, when these were not forthcoming, terrorism was employed to enforce collection. Atrocities at the hands of irresponsible company employees forced an investigation directed by de Brazza in person in 1905. While the commission's report was suppressed, flagrant abuses were remedied by Gentil and his successors and most of the concessions had been abandoned by 1914.

Wild rubber, ivory and wood were the chief products. Trade rose from eighteen million francs in 1900 to fifty-eight million in 1913. It was, however, largely in British and German hands. Gentil and Libreville became ports of some consequence. On the outbreak of war, French Equatorial Africa's resources had barely been tapped and little had been done for the natives save in a medical way. Its potentialities were nevertheless great and it was consequently termed the "Cinderella" of the Gallic family.

FRENCH SOMALILAND

France's failure to secure the upper Nile Valley through the Marchand Expedition ended the dream of creating a vast trans-African domain extending from the Red Sea to the Atlantic and left French Somaliland isolated. The colony nevertheless assumed considerable importance in the new century. With the development of French Asia and Oceania, Djibouti, the only French port of call en route, underwent rapid growth. Construction of the Abyssinian Railway, a French enterprise, between 1897 and 1914, diverted most of the old caravan traffic through adjacent territories to French Somaliland. Imports rose from six million francs in 1900 to 28.5 million in 1913 and exports from seven hundred thousand francs to 43.6 million in the same years.

The long-disputed northwestern boundary was set by Franco-Italian protocols of 1900 and 1901. The old name, Obock, was dropped in 1902. Coffee cultivation made considerable progress after 1905 and rich salt mines were opened in 1912. A mission school dating from 1902 did much to foster cordial relations with the natives.

MADAGASCAR

Madagascar's conversion into a colony in 1896, following Queen Rànavàlona III's (r. from 1883; d. 1917) attempt to destroy the protectorate and regain her independence, was followed by an entire reconstruction of Malagash life. General Joseph Galliéni (1849-1916) who had crushed the insurrection remained as Governor-General. He deposed and exiled the queen, destroyed the Hova people's supremacy, restored tribal autonomy, abrogated royalty, emancipated the slaves, converted feudal tenures into petty proprietorships and abolished forced labor. Free land grants were offered French settlers and irreconcilable Boers were accorded refuge following their defeat in the South African War. Highways and a railroad were constructed, mining concessions were granted, finances were reorganized and tariffs were erected against non-French goods. Upon Galliéni's retirement in 1905, the island had been thoroughly pacified and rapid economic progress was under way.

Victor Augagneur, the new Governor-General (r. 1905-1910), aroused bitter resentment by interfering with native religious customs. A new policy of placing all tribes under the direct control of French officials and subjecting them to constant French influence, inaugurated by his successor Albert Picquié in 1910, likewise occasioned hostility. A powerful nationalist movement consequently appeared and derived additional impetus from the institution of compulsory education. It had made marked headway by 1914 and was destined to cause endless complications during the World War.

French rule brought material prosperity. Ranching, gold and graphite mining, sericulture and rubber and cotton planting became important industries. Foreign trade rose from 50 million francs in 1900 to 104 million in 1913. The population increased from 2.2 million in 1901 to 3.1 million a decade later; the number of French residents from 1,200 to 13,000. Most of the best soil, however, passed to the Europeans. In 1914, 1,900,000 acres of cultivated land were in the hands of 16,000 whites while more than 3,000,000 natives held but 2,300,000 acres. Alcoholism and tuberculosis were both then ravaging the country.

In 1912 the insular protectorates of Anjouan, Grande Comore and Moheli and the adjacent colony of Mayotte, in the Mozambique Channel, were converted into Comoro Islands Colony which was attached to Madagascar. Vanilla formed its principal export.

REUNION

This highly-developed island—"a bit of the motherland in African waters"—was the greatest sugar-producing area within the French Empire at the turn of the century. Its population had virtually stabilized at 175,000 and almost all arable land was under cultivation. Following the glutting of European markets with beet sugar and a disastrous hurricane which bankrupted many planters in 1904, primitive methods of sugar manufacturing were abandoned in favor of central mills and refineries. Increasing attention was likewise paid to vanilla production. While imports shrank from 22 million to 12.7 million francs between 1900 and 1914, exports continued at some 17.5 million and the ruin confronting the colony a decade earlier was averted. Reunion's trade was almost exclusively in Gallic hands; its civilization was wholly French. On the eve of war, it was commonly hailed as France's most successful colony.

AMERICA

France's New World possessions in 1900 were mere fragments of the great trans-Atlantic empire erected during the seventeenth and eighteenth centuries. While insignificant in extent compared to Britain's American colonies, they nevertheless occupied positions of considerable importance in the French economic structure.

ST. PIERRE AND MIQUELON

St. Pierre and Miquelon, off the mouth of the St. Lawrence, were the center of France's seafood industry, but declining prices lowered the value of exports from 12.2 million francs in 1900 to six million in 1913. Heavy emigration followed, the population sank by one-third (only 4,000 islanders remained in 1913) and codfishing, the chief occupation, fell into the hands of homeland crews coming out for a season's catch. But 24 local smacks were operating in 1914, one-eighth the number registered at the start of the century. Insular business houses and the colonial Government were both in financial difficulties after 1905. Loss of revenue forced the contraction of a five million franc loan and, for reasons of economy, the Governor was replaced in 1906 by an administrator. Economic and social conditions on the eve of the War were generally deplorable.

GUADELOUPE AND MARTINIQUE

Guadeloupe and Martinique, long the sugar-bowls of the Empire, were now likewise producing coffee and cacao in abundance. Large tracts of fresh land were opened about 1900 and coolie immigration attained considerable proportions. Cacao production in Guadeloupe trebled between 1900 and 1913 (2.4 million lbs. in the latter year) while the number of sugar works in Martinique doubled (35 in 1913). The foreign trade of each remained stationary at some fifty million francs a year.

The population of Guadeloupe rose from 172,000 in 1901 to 212,500 in 1912. Martinique suffered one of the greatest natural disasters of history in 1902 when Mont Pelée erupted, destroying St. Pierre, the metropolis, and snuffing out 40,000 lives. The population, which had stood at 190,000 in the late 1890's, nevertheless passed 195,000 by 1913. Such rapid increase and a marked overbalance of females posed serious social problems in both islands. The construction of the Panama Canal in this period gave them great strategic value.

FRENCH GUIANA

French Guiana's long-standing boundary dispute with Brazil was at length settled in 1900 by a Swiss arbitration court, named for the purpose, which drew the line at the Oyapock River and the Tumucumaque Mountains. As for two generations past, its use as a penal colony seriously retarded its development. The malodorous Dreyfus Affair focused world attention on the colony early in the new century and enhanced its sinister reputation to such an extent that free immigration was almost non-existent by 1913. The population maintained itself at some 49,000, though the number of convicts rose from 7,000 to 8,500.

Cultivation remained static at 8,000 acres. Gold production was the chief industry, the output rising from 82,000 oz. in 1899 to 128,000 in 1912. Largely because of this, exports rose from six to ten million francs in the interim while imports continued at about ten million. Such external trade fell largely to France. The rosewood industry, now of major importance, dates from 1900. Settlement of the Inini highland by assisted immigration and abolition of the penal system were both under serious discussion in 1914 but nothing had been undertaken to either end. Railway construction had barely begun. Thus, at the outbreak of war, Guiana still lay largely unexplored with its resources largely untouched.

ASIA

THE FRENCH ESTABLISHMENTS IN INDIA

The five cities Chandarnagar, Yanaon, Pondicherry, Karikal and Mahé forming the colony of French India had become much more than standing sources of annoyance to the British by the turn of the century. As integral parts of Hindustan, they shared in the latter's rapid development. Pondicherry, in particular, underwent rapid industrialization—its output of textiles (chiefly cotton and jute) doubled between 1900 and 1914. Possession of these ports facilitated intercourse with the entire area and their foreign trade, which was chiefly in French hands, rose from fifteen million to forty-two million francs in our period. For this practical, as well as for sentimental reasons, the homeland attached great store to the Establishments in India and declined to exchange these remote possessions for Gambia during negotiations leading to the Entente Cordiale.

INDOCHINA

France's several holdings in the Malay Peninsula—the colony of Cochin China and the protectorates of Cambodia, Annam, Laos and Tonkin—were united in 1898 to form the Indochinese Union. Kwang-Chow-Wan, which was acquired under a 99-year lease from China in the same year, was attached to the Union in 1900. Two cessions of Siamese territory in 1904 and 1907 rectifying the western boundary gave Indochina its present form.

This territorial consolidation was accompanied by administrative and fiscal unification. The Governor-General was accorded wide authority and became the most powerful official within France's colonial Empire. Paul Doumer (1857-1932), holding office from 1897-1902, filled the post with signal success. A common budget was introduced, public works projects were centralized, a single court of appeal was established and an integrated railroad system, giving the Union one of the best networks of communication in Asia, was inaugurated. The customs union dating from 1887 was, of course, continued.

Such institution of uniform direction was followed by marked economic advance. While few settlers came out from the metropole, Indochina now became a popular field for investment. Rice, tea, cotton and rubber plantations were laid out in the lush Mekong, Black and Red River valleys. Sericulture likewise made rapid strides. Coal, lignite and zinc deposits were opened. Teakwood found a ready market in France. Textile mills and metallurgical plants were likewise set up in large number and their low overhead enabled French industrialists to compete successfully with Japan throughout the Orient. Labor was provided by the sedentary Malay and Chinese populations.

Chinese immigration, a conspicuous social phenomenon in the area for half a century, increased with the growth of economic opportunity. By 1914 much of the best land and petty shopkeeping had fallen into their hands. The cities of Hanoi, Hue and Saigon enjoyed mushroom growth and the first now won the name of "the Paris of the East". A serious effort was made to Gallicize the inhabitants and the use of French throughout the entire school system was receiving serious consideration on the eve of the War.

By 1914 Indochina had become the jewel of the French Empire and the post of Governor-General had become a stepping-stone to the Ministry of Colonies.

OCEANIA

France's scattered South Pacific possessions—the Society Islands, the Marquesas, the Tuamotus, the Leewards, Gambier, Tubuai and Rapa—were merged in 1903 to form the colony of French Establishments in Oceania with Papeete on Tahiti in the Society group as its capital.

The new century found these islands in economic transition. Cotton, tobacco and coffee planting were giving way to copra production which rapidly became the leading industry. America formed the chief market and by 1914 engrossed the greater part of French Oceania's trade. The indigenous Polynesians progressively disappeared before the onslaught of European diseases, alcoholism and alien ways of life. An acute labor shortage resulted and was met by importing indentured Malays from Indochina.

French Oceania was well-known in artistic circles by 1914 through Paul Gauguin's (1848-1903) spectacular canvasses depicting all phases of native life. The South Sea cult, destined to attain tremendous vogue in the post-war era, had its roots in this earlier age.

The transportation of criminals to New Caledonia ceased in 1896 and by 1914 less than 3,000 persons of convict origin remained in the island. Abolition of the penal system gave marked impetus to the colony's development. A considerable influx of free settlers from France and Indochina followed and numerous plantations were laid out in the land-grant area. The immigrants conducted interesting experiments with wheat, rubber and silk, but coffee and sugar continued the main agricultural crops. The labor problem was met by recruiting indentured hands on adjacent French islands. Ranching was stimulated by the award of a French army contract to a local meat-packing syndicate.

Mining was, however, the basic industry of the pre-war period. New Caledonia contained one of the few known deposits of nickel as well as large beds of cobalt, manganese and other industrial ores. These were worked by French corporations which erected blast furnaces and marketed most of their product in the United

States. Nickel shipments alone comprised two-thirds the total exports in 1914 (then valued at 15 million francs). From 1900 to 1914 France enjoyed but one-quarter of the colony's trade and economic ties steadily bound it closer to the United States. Wallis and Futuna, insular dependencies of New Caledonia, became important coffee, cotton and copra producing areas early in the new century.

The establishment of an Anglo-French condominium over the New Hebrides archipelago in 1906 failed to stabilize that community. Investors shunned the area and constant bickering between the French and British colonists continued. It soon became apparent that the experiment was not a success, and as early as 1914 a joint Anglo-French committee was named to survey the situation and recommend changes. It had not reported on the outbreak of war. Throughout the period 1898-1914, many thousand islanders were recruited to serve as indentured laborers in New Caledonia.

Title to Clipperton Island, 800 miles off the Mexican coast, was long disputed between France and Mexico. The King of Italy was at length chosen as arbiter in 1908 and ultimately awarded it to France in 1931. The factors behind this protracted and entirely unreasonable delay have never been made clear.

FRANCE

Unlike in Great Britain, there was scant enthusiasm for empire building in France before 1914. The population was stationary and emigration was slight. The few individuals leaving their homeland showed singular disinclination to settle in the colonies and generally speaking only misfits, lured by free passage and generous land grants, took up residence there. Investors, too, preferred placing their capital in Russia, the Americas or the British Empire. Credits were grudgingly voted and parliamentary indifference repeatedly blocked expansion. So great was popular apathy that Delcassé, the far-sighted Minister of Colonies who sought to incorporate Morocco within the Empire, was sacrificed in 1905 to meet German objections to his program. The dismemberment of French Equatorial Africa in 1911 to conciliate Germany likewise failed to rouse the nation.

Colonial trade never formed more than a fraction of France's external commerce. In the decade ending 1903, it reached but 10.49 per cent of the total. In 1904 imports from her dependencies reached only 487 million francs (10.82 per cent of the total) and exports 558 million francs (12.54 per cent of the same). In 1913 France's entire Empire trade amounted to a mere 1,692,000,000 francs—11 per cent of the total. Indeed the foreign commerce of the French colonies before the Great War was chiefly in British and German hands.

A vigorous campaign to foster imperial sentiment was, however, in progress. This was conducted by the Comité de l'Afrique Française (founded in 1890), the Comité de Madagascar (1895), the Comité de l'Asie Française (1901) and the Comité de l'Océanie Française (1904), whose members comprised industrialists, shippers and bankers with colonial interests, and returned officials and missionaries. These bodies were indefatigable in arranging public lectures, staging colonial exhibits and sponsoring popular treatises on Greater France. Newspapers and periodicals, such as *L'Action Coloniale* (1904) and *La Revue Indigène* (1906), devoted to colonial life and interests, were likewise founded in considerable number.

Expansionist propaganda stressed France's civilizing mission, the importance of overseas possessions as markets and sources of supply for raw products, the stimulus they accorded Christianization, their value as reservoirs of manpower to meet military needs, the economic opportunity they provided, the safety of investments under the tricolor and the symbolic significance of colonies as gauges of national prestige. Fervid appeals were made to Gallic pride and patriotism. "France's Empire is greater than all other empires, save only the British, combined. Greater France is now a nation 100,000,000 strong." In his *Fecundity* (1899), Emile Zola (1840-1920) envisaged hardy French pioneers spreading to the ends of the earth and perpetuating the glories of the motherland in distant lands.

Such efforts were not wholly barren of results. The "Greater France" concept attained a certain vogue in intellectual circles. The study of French expansion was inaugurated in homeland schools, and courses in colonial geography, history, economics and law were introduced in the leading universities. Some popular interest in the Empire developed and a few adventurers resorted to the colonies to employ their talents in a more favorable environment than that afforded by the metropole. However, despite such activities, the French as a whole were still in 1914 "little Frenchmen," viewing the colonies as strange lands "far away, down there in the bright sunshine." Empire feeling, today such an important force in French life, was largely born of the Great War and the reconstruction years.

Chapter IV

The German Colonial Empire
AFRICA

TOGOLAND

TOGOLAND won distinction in the period 1898-1914 through becoming the only self-supporting portion of German Africa. These years brought steady progress. Final boundary adjustments were made with Great Britain in 1899 and with France in 1899 and 1911. The European population rose from 125 to 375, of whom most were German plantation managers, traders and missionaries. Shipping facilities were provided at Lome. Two railroads were constructed from that port to Palime and Atakpame in the interior and another along the coast to Anekho. Some 200 miles of track and 750 miles of motor roads had opened the southern third of the country in 1914. The hinterland was, as yet, undeveloped because of poor communication.

Palm, coffee, cacao and kolanut estates were laid out and tobacco, cotton and rubber production were undertaken with a fair degree of success. Palm kernels were, at all times, the chief crop. External trade, which was monopolized by the Germans, rose from 6.5 million marks in 1900 to 19.8 million in 1913. Some 15,000 native children were receiving practical education along agricultural, mechanical and domestic lines in 1913.

KAMERUN

Kamerun, a tropical wilderness, remained the least developed portion of Teutonic Africa. The Chad shore was not occupied until 1902 and adequate river outlets were not secured until 1911 when, in connection with the Moroccan settlement, France ceded two portions of French Equatorial Africa which afforded Kamerun access to the Congo and the Ubangi. Anglo-German agreements of 1906 and 1913 at length determined the western boundary.

Only the area about Mt. Kamerun in the west was developed by 1914. Less than 2,000 whites then resided there. Plantation enterprises were largely in the hands of concession corporations. The Northwestern Kamerun Company alone held 35,000 square miles. But the native population was small and labor shortages were chronic; a mere 55,000 acres were under cultivation in the entire colony in 1914. Cacao and rubber were the chief plantation crops. The forests yielded wild rubber and palm products, and ivory was an important export item. Gold and iron had been located but the deposits lay untouched for lack of capital. Less than 200 miles of railway were in operation. Despite Kamerun's primitive state, some progress was made—external trade rose from 16 million marks to 63.7 million in the period 1900-1913.

Arbitrary acts by Governor von Puttkamer brought on serious native disorders in 1904-1905. His recall and dismissal improved relations and by 1914 harmony had been restored. Mission schools proved a potent factor in cementing the tie. Compulsory education for native children was instituted in 1910 and there were 40,000 in actual attendance on the eve of war—one of the largest groups in any European exploitation colony.

GERMAN SOUTHWEST AFRICA

Considerable development followed pacification of the country in 1894. Under Governor Theodor von Leutwein (r. 1894-1904), "the father of German Southwest Africa," loans were made to approved settlers, refugee Boers were admitted in large number, a harbor was constructed at Swakopmund, copper mines were opened in the north, ranching became well established, a road was mapped through the narrow outlet to the Zambezi, two railroads were completed and another was projected. Despite its suitability for European settlement in certain spots, there were less than 5,000 whites in the colony by 1904. This was due to the presence of powerful groups of natives such as the Hottentots and the Hereros, to the heavy capital outlays needed for exploitation and to excessive land grants to concession concerns made by the home Government. In 1903, nine corporations controlled one-third of the entire area. One concern alone, the Southwestern Africa Colonial Company, owned all the coast.

Encroachments on native land inevitably led to conflict. The Herero War, opening in 1904, was one of the most sanguinary in colonial history. General von Trotha, a stiff-necked militarist sent out from Germany, undertook to exterminate the blacks. His savagery led to his recall but peace was not effected until his successor, Governor Friedrich von Lindequist, threw 19,000 men into action. The conflict ended in 1908 after costing 100,000 native lives—one-half the African population—and 700 million marks.

Extensive tracts were then thrown open to settlers. The discovery of diamonds in 1908 in the vicinity of Luderitz Bay brought an inrush of adventurers and by 1913 there were 15,000 Europeans in the colony. External trade, which had stood at 10 million marks in 1899, rose to 113.7 million by 1913. The colony, was, however, still operated at a loss mounting to 39 million marks in 1913.

GERMAN EAST AFRICA

The high hopes for the rapid development of this large and rich colony were not realized in the pre-war period. While the inland plateaus were ideally suited for European residence, the number of whites had barely reached 5,000 by 1914 and exploitation had only begun. This arose from two causes—the East African Company's strangle hold on the economic life of the area and native hostility.

The East African Company had resolved itself into a private commercial concern upon the home Government's assumption of political control in German East Africa in 1891. It held title to large blocks of land, controlled the forests, received a half-interest in all mining concessions and enjoyed priority rights in railroad construction. When, at the turn of the century, it built a line running inland from Tanga, it received a belt of land 3½ miles wide along the right of way plus 12,000 acres of land elsewhere for each mile of track completed. The private settler consequently found little scope for his talents.

Governmental solicitude for native welfare, as revealed by decrees of 1901-1905 mitigating slavery, emancipating all newly-born children and gradually abolishing serfdom, and by the establishment of numerous schools and hospitals, was, unhappily, nullified by arbitrary acts of bureaucratic officials and by systematic encroachments on native lands. Some 7.5 million blacks under capable leaders already occupied the best land. Incessant conflict over titles at length culminated in a great uprising in 1905-1906 which took 120,000 African lives. A law of 1907, prohibiting the sale to white settlers of land already occupied by natives, did much to conciliate the latter but materially hindered development.

The ultimate extension of the Northern Railroad, terminating at Tanga, to New Moshi, 220 miles in the interior, and the construction of the Central Railway (780 miles) from Dar-es-Salaam, on the coast, to Ujiji, on Lake Tanganyika, in the years immediately preceding the War, as well as the frank adoption of British colonial methods after 1907, bode well for the future. But little had been accomplished by the outbreak of hostilities and the colony still ran a 41 million mark deficit in 1913—the largest for any portion of the Empire. External trade rose from 16 million marks in 1900 to 89 million in 1913, with rubber, coffee, sisal, ivory, cotton and copra as the chief exports. Native education made conspicuous progress—some 2,000 government and mission schools were in operation in 1914 with 108,000 children enrolled.

ASIA

The murder of two German missionaries in Shantung Province in November 1897 afforded Germany the welcome opportunity of securing a foothold along the Chinese coast. When troops were landed, the Chinese Government speedily (March

1898) accorded a 99-year lease on Kiaochow Bay (some 200 square miles along the eastern shore of the Shantung Peninsula), created a 2,500 sq. m. neutral zone around it and granted German interests railroad and mining concessions in the vicinity.

Tsingtao, on Kiaochow Bay, was converted into a powerfully fortified naval base. A free port was set up in 1899 and the leased district soon handled an important share of the north China trade. The first railroad opened in 1901 by 1914, 270 miles of line were in operation. Large numbers of natives were induced to sell land to the German Government which, in turn, resold it to its nationals. The resident white population in 1914 consequently stood at 4,500. Exports in 1913 reached 79.6 million marks and imports six million. But Kiaochow's chief value arose from the prestige its possession brought Germany throughout the Far East and the facilities it afforded the German Pacific fleet for dockage, coaling and provisioning. The heavy annual deficit (10.3 million marks in 1913) was not, consequently, begrudged.

THE PACIFIC BASIN

The triple protectorate over the Samoan Islands established by Great Britain, the United States and Germany in 1889 gave way to a new arrangement in 1899-1900. The kingship was now abolished, Great Britain withdrew from the group and accepted certain of the German Solomon Islands by way of compensation, Germany took possession of Savaii and Upolu and the United States acquired Tutuila.

Native rights were carefully safeguarded in German Samoa. Land could be acquired only in a restricted district under stringent conditions and the granting of credit to indigenes was proscribed. Two thousand indentured Chinese were imported as plantation hands. Some 8,000 acres were under cultivation in 1914 with copra and cacao as the chief crops. Apia developed rapidly as a port. German Samoa's external trade, which was largely in Australian hands, rose from four to ten million marks between 1900 and 1913.

Corporation rule, which had survived longer in Oceania than in Africa, now likewise suffered inglorious failure there. The New Guinea Company yielded its administrative rights in Kaiser Wilhelm's Land (German New Guinea), the Bismarck Archipelago and the German Solomons in 1899 but continued to operate as a private concern. Other companies laid out extensive coconut, cacao, cotton and rubber properties. Nearly 50,000 acres were under cultivation by 1914, and exports, which had stood at 3 million marks in 1900, reached 11 million in 1913. The Jaluit Company in the Marshall Islands surrendered its charter in 1906 and the group was thereupon attached to Kaiser Wilhelm's Land.

Spain's defeat in the Spanish-American War was followed by Germany's purchase of the remaining Iberian Islands—the Carolines, the Pelews and the Mariannes (Ladrones)—for 16.75 million marks in 1899. The Marshalls and these later acquisitions had a combined white population of only 450 in 1913. Their external trade then reached 10.3 million marks, with copra and phosphate as the basic products.

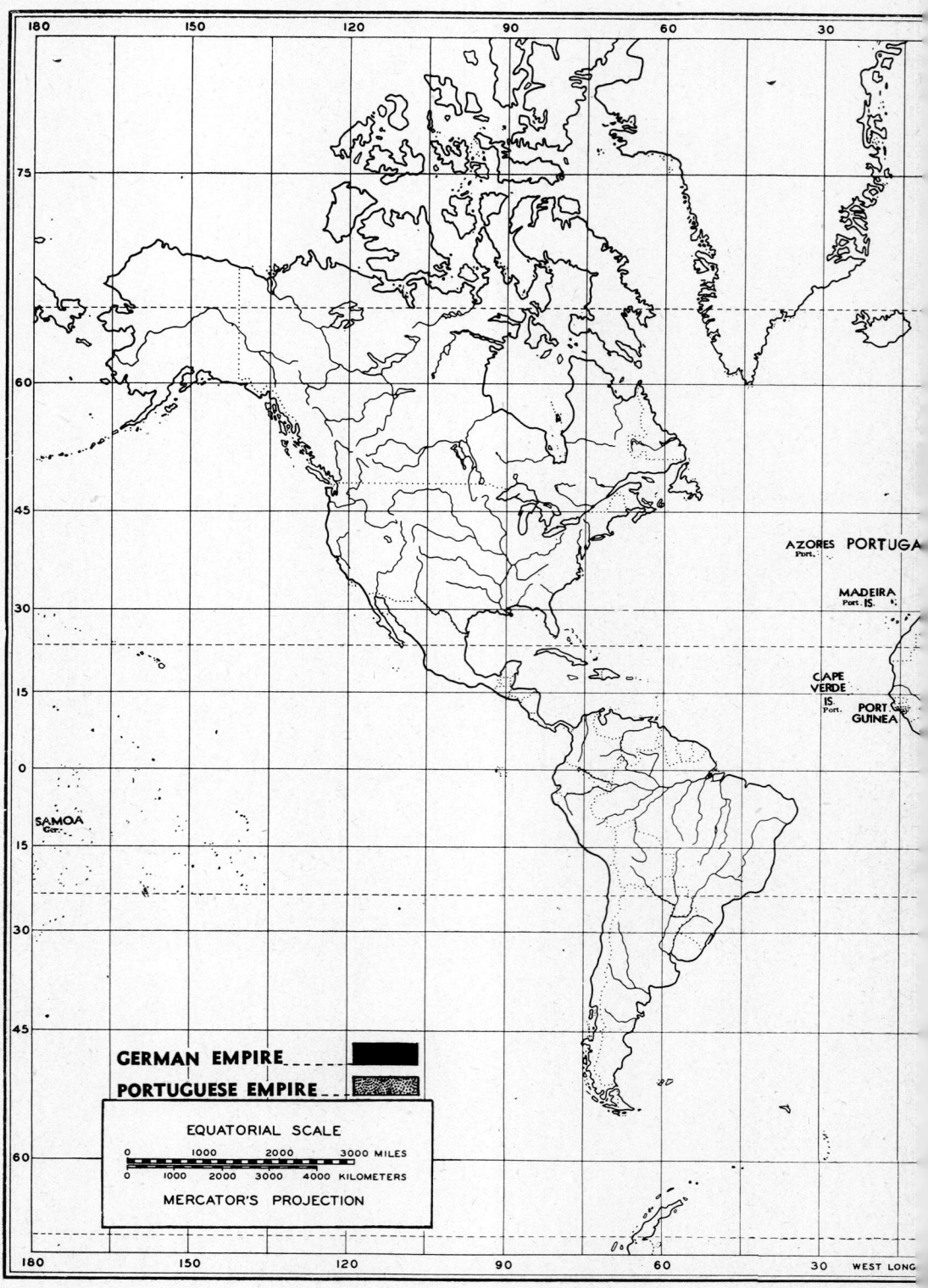

The German and

GERMANY

Kiaochow
Ger.

Macao
Port.

GOA
Port.

MARIANAS
Ger.

MARSHALL
IS.
Ger.

CAROLINE
IS.
Ger.

PELEW
IS.

GER. NEW GUINEA
BISMARK ARCH.
SOLOMON IS.

TIMOR
Port.

KAMERUN

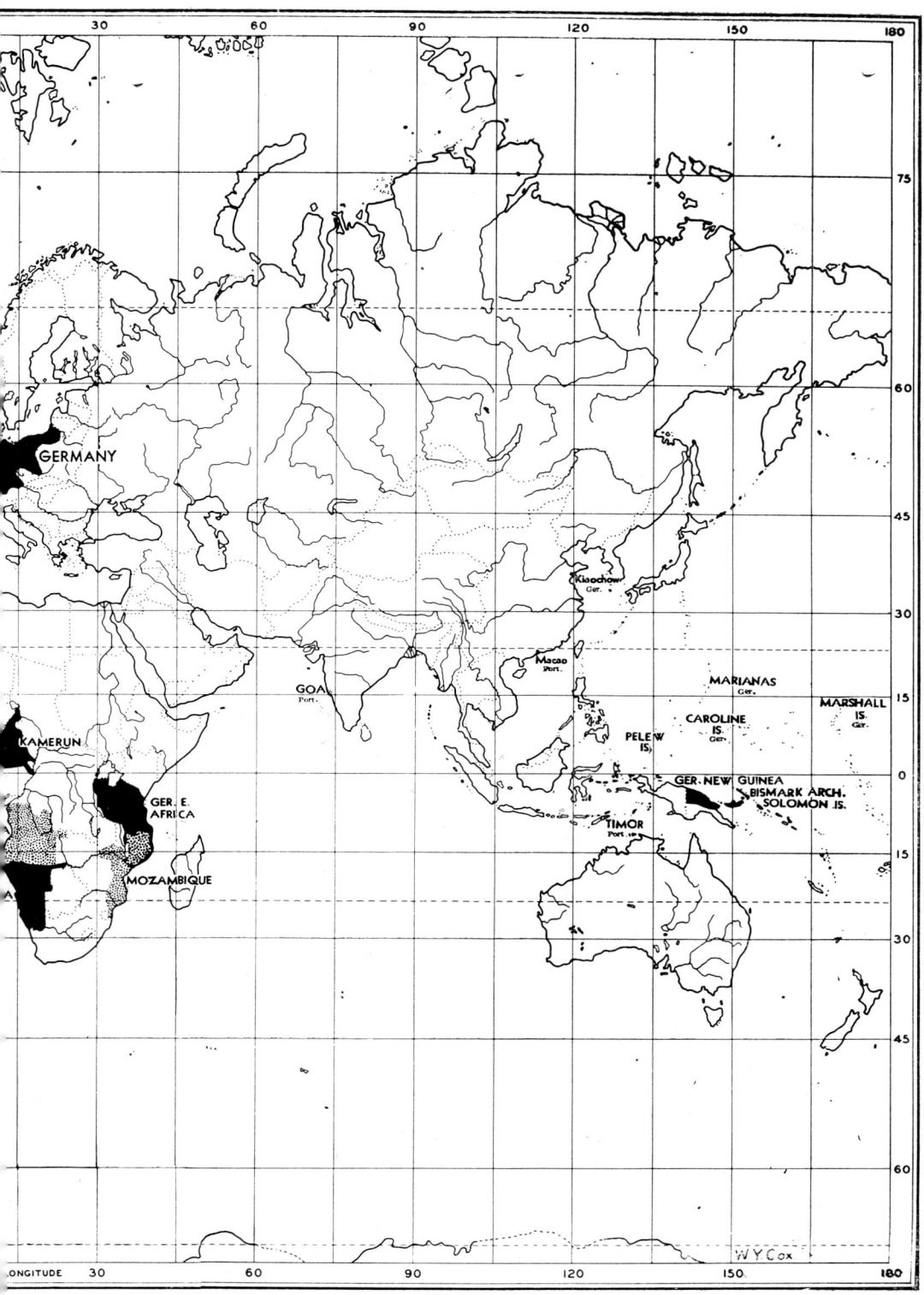

GER. E.
AFRICA

MOZAMBIQUE

W Y Cox

LONGITUDE 30   60   90   120   150   180

mpires in 1914

GERMANY

The German Government was thoroughly committed to an imperialistic program by the late 1890's. Colonial expansion formed an integral part of William II's (b. 1859; r. 1888-1918) policy in steering "the new course." Overseas holdings were desired not merely as markets, sources of supply for raw products, places of settlement for emigrants and fields for investment but because they symbolized world power. As a great people, declared the eloquent Chancellor von Bülow (1849-1929), the Germans must have their "place in the sun."

The disintegration of China made possible the acquisition of Kiaochow in 1898. Spain's Pacific possessions were attracting great attention just prior to the Spanish-American War. The dispatch of a German fleet to Manila Bay and the Emperor's suggestion that a division of Spanish territory be effected by America and Germany (1898) bore no fruit but, following the restoration of peace, Spain's remaining islands were purchased in 1899. An Anglo-German convention of 1898 provided that, should Portugal default on a proposed loan from those two countries with certain of her colonial revenues serving as security, Germany was to secure southern Angola (adjoining German Southwest Africa), northern Mozambique (adjacent to German East Africa) and Timor in the East Indies. German Samoa emerged some months later (1899).

The British conquest of the Boer Republics (1899-1902) ended hopes of creating German protectorates over the Orange Free State and the Transvaal and the challenge to France in Morocco (1905-1911) brought only certain trading rights there (1909) and two river outlets for Kamerun (1911). However, a second Anglo-German treaty drafted in 1913-1914 and already initialled before the outbreak of war promised important tangibilities. This agreement envisaged the early dismemberment of Portuguese Africa and Germany's acquisition of all of Angola save the remote interior, as well as northern Mozambique and St. Thomas and Prince's Islands in the Guinea Gulf.

Economic dominion was meanwhile being gained over Asiatic Turkey through the Bagdad Railway. A visit paid the Sultan by the Kaiser in 1898 yielded German interests a concession to extend the existing Anatolian line in Asia Minor to the banks of the Tigris. This aroused tremendous resentment, especially in Great Britain, which felt her hold on India imperilled. But work had been largely completed when, in June 1914, British opposition was withdrawn in return for a share in the enterprise and the recognition of Britain's preponderant position in Mesopotamia. A branch was meanwhile run southward through Syria, Palestine and Arabia, extending German influence in those areas.

These imperialistic adventures by no means enjoyed the unanimous support of the German people. Both the Center and Socialist parties were highly vocal in their opposition. Governor von Puttkamer's misgovernment in the Kamerun, scandals involving the concession companies, the perpetual deficits and the costly native wars in Kamerun, Southwest Africa and East Africa were fully exploited. Obstructionist tactics in the Reichstag reached such heights in 1906 that von Bülow dissolved the body and ordered new elections. Colonial empire was the clear-cut issue. Government agencies placed heavy pressure on the voters and, in the balloting of

January 1907, the Emperor's expansionist program scored a tremendous victory.

Notable consequences followed this parliamentary crisis. A Colonial Department was established in 1906 with Bernhard Dernburg (1865-1937), a financier, in charge. A year later it became the Ministry of Colonies. Overseas administration was promptly reorganized, the concession system was undermined, native interests were accorded protection and an attempt was made to unify the Empire economically. These policies were continued by Dernburg's successors, Dr. Friedrich von Lindequist (1910-1911) and Dr. Wilhelm Solf (1911-1918). The turn had come by 1914; the eve of war found the colonies firmly rooted and enjoying general support among the German people.

The future appeared bright indeed. Native resistance had been overcome, there were then 24,000 Germans residing in the colonies, investments there had risen from 185 million marks to more than 550 million in the past decade, railroad mileage had risen ten fold, trade had quadrupled and the area under cultivation had trebled. But Germany's colonial trade still formed less than one-half per cent of her entire commerce and the overseas possessions were still operated at a 100 million mark loss in 1913. German expansion had, consequently, barely begun to justify itself before the breaking of the storm.

Chapter V

The Portuguese Empire
AFRICA

UNDER the impetus of substantial British and German investments, Portuguese Africa[1] made rapid strides in the new century. The Cape Verde archipelago alone failed to share in this general movement because of heavy emigration to Cape Cod and California.

ST. THOMAS AND PRINCE'S ISLANDS

St. Thomas and Prince's Islands proved ideally suited for coffee and cacao production. Coffee yield reached a peak of 4 million pounds in 1902 but cacao became the primary crop shortly after. By 1913, when exports reached nearly 40,000 tons, these islands had become the second most important cacao producing area in the world, their output being surpassed only by that of nearby British Gold Coast. Indentured hands were imported from the Cape Verdes and the mainland possessions when the local labor supply proved inadequate but weak control caused the system to degenerate into slavery of the worst type. Numerous officials were involved in the scandal and in 1909 British and German chocolate manufacturers refused to purchase further supplies unless the entire contract regime were overhauled. Vigorous action by home authorities led to basic reforms and salvaged the industry.

GUINEA

Guinea, an enclave in French West Africa, received its present boundaries through demarcation by a Franco-Portuguese commission between 1902 and 1905. Rubber and oil nuts formed the chief products. The colony's trade fell progressively into Teutonic hands and by 1914 Germany dominated its economic life. Native disorders culminated in 1908 in a bloody war which subjected Portugal's colonial methods to widespread criticism.

---

[1] The Azores and the Madeiras have long been integral parts of Portugal.

ANGOLA

Angola attained its pre-war limits in 1905 when Victor Emmanuel III (1869-) of Italy defined the disputed Rhodesian frontier under an Anglo-Portuguese arbitration agreement. Construction of the Benguela Railway, a British line providing an outlet through Angola for the Katanga copper mines in southern Belgian Congo, was begun in 1904 and led to heavy German settlement in the interior. The thriving port, Lobito, was founded in 1905 to serve as its coastal terminus. Six hundred miles of track in four localities were laid between 1900 and 1914. Plantations, which were chiefly German-owned, now appeared in large number and coffee, oil nuts and cotton replaced wild rubber and ivory as basic export commodities. Petroleum and asphalt beds were likewise opened by British interests.

Angola provided St. Thomas and Prince's Islands with most of their indentured workers and the colony's officials were heavily involved in contract abuses. Both tribal slavery and the slave trade survived in many districts and forced labor was employed on public works. Kabinda, a separate possession across the narrow coastal stretch of Belgian Congo from Angola and administered from the latter, continued stagnant because of its isolation.

PORTUGUESE EAST AFRICA

Portuguese East Africa enjoyed the heaviest influx of foreign capital in this period. The Mozambique Company, a chartered corporation holding sovereign rights over the territory between 22° south latitude and the lower reaches of the Zambezi almost to its mouths (Domains of the Mozambique Company) from 1891 to 1941 and whose stock was largely British-owned, opened plantations and mines on a lavish scale. The transit trade from Rhodesia to the port of Beira, the Company's administrative center, via the Beira Railroad, suffered a temporary decline upon the opening of rail communication between Rhodesia and the Cape in 1902 but was revived by lower rates and attained unprecedented proportions by 1914. The Nyasa Company, a concern with many German stockholders exercising administrative and economic control from 1894 to 1929 over the lands between the Lurio River and German East Africa, undertook the methodical development of that region. Its capital, Porto Amelia, now became a bustling metropolis.

Mozambique Province, which embraced the two sections of Portuguese East Africa administered directly by the state, was reconstructed in 1907 to facilitate intelligent exploitation. It was divided into five districts (Lourenço Marques, Inhambane, Quelimane, Tete and Mozambique), each with distinct economic interests and each headed by a Governor empowered to make liberal land grants and mining concessions. Foreign capital now quickly poured into Mozambique Province. The city of Lourenço Marques, which had become the Transvaal's chief outlet upon completion of the Delagoa Bay Railroad in 1895, served Swaziland in similar fashion after the construction of a new line to the protectorate in 1910. The Mozambique Convention of 1909, regulating such transit commerce, proved highly advantageous to the Portuguese and made Lourenço Marques a leading African port. In 1907 it replaced Mozambique City as the provincial capital.

Large-scale Hindu immigration into all parts of Portuguese East Africa set in at the close of the nineteenth century and by 1914 local trade was largely in Indian hands. Conversely, many natives emigrated from Mozambique Province as contract laborers either to the cacao estates of St. Thomas or to the Transvaal goldfields. Missionary societies, chiefly foreign and Protestant, expanded their work rapidly in the new century and their admirable native schools materially lessened the shock arising from the impact of new forces.

While incomplete statistics and currency depreciation make exact comparison impossible, Portuguese Africa's foreign trade, exclusive of transit shipments, appears to have increased about one-half between 1898 and 1914 with cacao, coffee, rubber, sugar and ivory forming the chief exports.

ASIA

Portuguese India (the cities of Goa, Daman and Diu, with their environs, on the west coast of the Hindustan peninsula) had fallen into complete stagnation by the early 1900's. Its glories of four centuries earlier had vanished, its trade was now largely a transit one and salt raking was the sole industry. Only its geographic position with respect to British India gave it importance.

Maçao, on the south China mainland at the mouth of the Canton River and another fragment of Portugal's old Far Eastern Empire, prospered greatly as a free port after the turn of the century. It now became the world center for the opium traffic. Licensed gambling drew adventurers from all quarters and by 1914 Maçao had won the dubious title of being "the wickedest spot on earth." The colony's business was almost exclusively in Chinese hands, the Portuguese themselves drawing scant profit from ownership.

Portuguese Timor (the eastern portion of Timor Island, in Melanesia, together with an enclave in Dutch Timor) had been detached from Maçao and converted into a separate colony in 1896. The delimitation of boundaries on the island, undertaken by a joint Portuguese-Dutch commission soon after, was not completed until 1914. Its isolation discouraged investment and it remained largely undeveloped in consequence. Its foreign trade on the eve of the War was less than 300,000 escudos (then approximately $250,000) and was carried on chiefly by the Dutch.

Alien influence had attained such proportions by 1914 that foreign rather than Portuguese coins were in general circulation throughout the Empire and accounts were commonly kept in pounds, marks or guilders.

PORTUGAL

Lack of resources and manpower prevented the decadent metropole from developing its overseas possessions. National bankruptcy in 1892 brought an abrupt halt to Portuguese investments and gave British, German, Indian, Chinese and Dutch capitalists complete ascendancy in the colonies by the early 1900's. Creation of the two East African chartered corporations and of innumerable concession companies at the turn of the century contributed materially to this unhealthy situation. What little immigration occurred to 1910 was almost exclusively foreign. Missionary activity was largely in British and German hands.

Home industries likewise proved incapable of consuming the colonies' produce. Existing law compelled the shipment of all commodities to Lisbon but most of them were immediately reexported. Trade restrictions bore grievously on the Empire and gave birth to a colonial self-government movement. This made rapid headway in the new century but was stoutly resisted lest Lisbon be ruined. Revolutionary agitation followed and by 1910 Angola and East Africa were seething with unrest.

Numerous reforms followed the emergence of the Republic in that year. Emigration to the colonies was fostered. The Roman Catholic Church was disestablished overseas. At length, in August 1914, the dependencies were accorded administrative and financial autonomy.

Portugal's incapacity as a colonial power was glaringly apparent by the close of the nineteenth century. The backward state of her territories, her maladministration and her iniquitous plantation regime were thoroughly publicized in the early 1900's. Anticipating her ultimate collapse, Germany and Great Britain had already delimited spheres of influence within her Empire in 1898. By joint agreement, southern Angola, northern Mozambique and Timor fell to the former and northern Angola and southern Mozambique to the latter. Each was to take over its zones should Portugal default on a proposed joint loan secured by the customs revenue of those colonies. A revised understanding followed in 1913-1914. All of Angola save an interior district, together with northern Mozambique, St. Thomas and Prince's Island, were now to fall to Germany as soon as possession might be gained in any manner, and eastern Angola, southern East Africa and Timor to Great Britain. This agreement had, however, not been ratified before the war crisis of 1914 and it lapsed on the outbreak of hostilities.

CHAPTER VI

The Italian Empire
AFRICA

ERITREA

CIVIL government was established in Eritrea in 1898 and the colony's boundaries were at length drawn by a series of agreements with Great Britain, France, Egypt and Abyssinia, negotiated between 1898 and 1908. Under Governor Ferdinando Martini (r. 1898-1906), the natives accepted Italian control, some 2,500 European immigrants came out as settlers and cotton planting became an important enterprise. Both the port of Massaua, handling transit commerce for Abyssinia and the Soudan as well as local trade, and the inland city of Asmara developed rapidly. The capital was shifted from Massaua to Asmara in 1900. A railroad connecting the two centers, completed twelve years later, gave access to the interior plateau. Trade rose from 13 million lire in 1900 to 32 million in 1913 with cotton, hides, palm nuts and mother-of-pearl forming the chief exports. Numerous concessions sought by foreign groups were uniformly denied and exploitation remained almost exclusively in Italian hands.

SOMALILAND

This territory, which had been administered and exploited by the Filonardi Company since 1892, was transferred to the Italian Benadir Corporation in 1898. The latter's charter accorded it a monopoly over land and mineral deposits together with an annual subsidy of 200,000 lire in return for governing the area. When the new concern proved equally incapable of coping with the situation, the Italian Government in 1905 purchased sovereign rights claimed by the Sultan of Zanzibar and assumed direct control. Considerable back country was acquired through a boundary convention with Abyssinia in 1908. The southern portion was converted into a Crown Colony two years later but the several northern protectorates survived until the middle 20's.

Colony and protectorates alike remained virtually undeveloped before the War. As harbors were entirely lacking, the small trade in hides and gum arabic was carried on from two tracts along Kismayu harbor in British East Africa, leased in 1905. The area's external commerce was a mere 10 million lire in 1913.

TRIPOLITANIA AND CYRENAICA

French designs on Morocco and Britain's need for clarifying her position in Egypt at length afforded Italy the opportunity to acquire a substantial portion of North Africa. Tripolitania and Cyrenaica, lying between Egypt and Tunis, held great potentialities. Italy had coveted both since suffering disappointment through France's establishment of the Tunisian protectorate. Now, in the new century, the drift of events placed them within her grasp.

Two conventions of 1900 and 1902 accorded her French support in exchange for a free hand in Morocco. Upon renewal of the Triple Alliance in 1902, a separate protocol assured her German and Austrian backing. Britain's approval was purchased in 1904 through recognizing her paramount position in Egypt. Russia's consent was won in 1909 by agreeing not to block her efforts at securing free use of the Dardanelles for her fleet. In the interim, Italian agents seduced tribesmen from their allegiance to the Turks, economic penetration was undertaken with the assistance of the Bank of Rome and the Bank of Italy, and a substantial Italian immigration set in.

Giovanni Giolitti (1842-1928), Premier from 1903 to 1905 and again from 1906 to 1909, was the directing force behind such activity and hoped to add both provinces to the Empire without conflict. But the Young Turk Revolution of 1908 made this impossible. These ardent Ottoman nationalists were bitterly hostile to Italian aspirations and favored German concessionnaires. Germany's setback in Morocco likewise raised the spectre of her seeking compensation elsewhere with Tripolitania-Cyrenaica the most likely area. Consequently, upon returning to power in 1911, Giolitti acted promptly lest Italy be forestalled here as she had been in Tunis. War was declared on Turkey on September 29, the coastal cities were captured, annexation followed in November and the ancient Roman name "Libya" was revived for the new colony.

When Turkey ignored such action and the war dragged on, Rhodes and the Dodecanese ("Twelve Islands") in the Aegean Sea were occupied and the Treaty of Lausanne followed in October 1912. Turkey now renounced her sovereignty over Tripolitania and Cyrenaica. Being on the brink of war with the Balkan Coalition, she sought to prevent a second loss of the islands by leaving them in Italy's hands as pledges for the early evacuation of the two provinces. All thirteen were ultimately ceded to Italy in 1923—an unexpected outcome of the North African adventure.

Libya was divided into two administrative districts, Tripolitania and Cyrenaica, with Tripoli and Bengazi as their respective capitals. Extreme difficulty was experienced in conquering the hinterland. Tripolitania's submission was complete by the outbreak of the First World War and serious efforts were being made to conciliate the natives. The interior of Cyrenaica was, however, still in the hands of the Senussites, a militant Moslem fraternity whose headquarters lay there and whose members had long battled the extension of Christian control throughout upper

The Italian Empire in 1914

Africa. Exploitation had, thus, barely opened by 1914. Libya's trade nevertheless reached 28.7 million lire in 1913—a bright promise for the future. Some 50 miles of railroad were already in operation a year later, numerous highways were under construction, two cables had been laid to Italy and assisted immigration had brought two thousand settlers to the colony. No attempt had, as yet, been made to develop the Aegean Islands because of the uncertainty respecting their ultimate disposition.

ITALY

When an Italian army seeking to conquer Abyssinia was virtually annihilated in the Adowa disaster of 1896, the greatest catastrophe in modern African history to that time, a popular revulsion against empire building arose throughout Italy. This carried over into the early 1900's.

Francesco Crispi (1819-1901), the expansionist Premier, was forced from office; Antonio Rudini (1839-1908), his successor (1896-1898), recognized Abyssinian independence and paid a heavy indemnity; and 138 members of the Italian Chamber of Deputies voted to abandon colonization entirely. Such progress as occurred overseas during the next decade was largely the work of two individuals, Governor Ferdinando Martini (1841-1928) in Eritrea and S. Filonardi, whose commercial corporation sought to develop Somaliland but collapsed in 1905. National opposition coupled with apathy lay behind Italy's failure to secure a sphere of influence in the San-Mun Bay area of China at the turn of the century to match British, German, Russian and French acquisitions of leased ports along the east coast.

A marked revival of interest in colonization developed about 1905 and attained such proportions that by 1914 it held the entire nation in its grip. This arose in part from a rapidly-growing population and the indignities suffered by Italian emigrants abroad, in part from a conviction that Italian prestige hinged upon exploits offsetting Adowa and in part from a strong nationalist movement then sweeping the country. The latter was the creation of a literary group headed by Enrico Coriadini (1865-1931), a popular novelist and journalist, whose two newspapers, *Regno* (1903) and *Ideanazionale* (1911), served as its leading organs. Such writings stressed Italy's Roman heritage, her mission of retrieving once-Roman lands from Turkish barbarism, the urgent need for an empire to care for Italy's teeming population and the increased international standing attending the ownership of colonies.

First fruits of the nationalist campaign were seen in the assumption of direct control over Somaliland in 1905 and the establishment of a Crown Colony there shortly after. Coriadini's articles on Tripolitania and Cyrenaica, following a visit in 1909, stirred the country to the depths. A nationalist congress, held at Florence in 1910, was so vocal in its demand for early action that Giolitti promptly launched war on Turkey upon his return to power. Only the Socialist Party opposed annexation of the two provinces and many of its members voting as individuals supported the Government in this action. Italian imperialism thus stood at full flood on the eve of the Great War.

Italy was, however, in no position to pursue an expansionist program. Her colonies were largely sterile and were capable of only limited expansion at great cost. The hold on northern Somaliland was loose and Cyrenaica as yet remained unconquered. This situation called for extensive military operations over an indefinite period. Less than 7,500 Italians had settled in all the colonies by 1914 whereas 285,000 emigrated to the United States alone in 1907. Likewise, her colonial trade between 1904 and 1913 totalled only 371 million lire—a mere three-fourths of one per cent of her external commerce. It is thus apparent that the Italian overseas possessions at the outbreak of the First World War enjoyed a sentimental value wholly disproportionate to their true worth.

CHAPTER VII

The Dutch Empire

THE CARIBBEAN AREA

AN influx of some 10,000 indentured Indians between 1898 and 1914 did much to solve the labor problem in Dutch Guiana (Surinam). Sugar production consequently rose from 21 to 33 million pounds. Cacao exports fell off by two-thirds (3,300,000 lbs. in 1914) due to plant epidemics but coffee planting made notable progress. Gold mining likewise expanded rapidly and the colony's production peak was reached in 1912 when 38,000 oz. were extracted. Foreign trade rose from 11.6 to 16.5 million guilders between 1898 and 1913. Budget deficits, however, increased from 20,000 to more than 800,000 guilders a year in the same period and became a steady drain on the home country's resources.

The Dutch West Indies (Curaçao and dependencies), too, were operated at a loss for a decade and a half before the World War, the deficit reaching 300,000 guilders in 1913. Agriculture stagnated. While small quantities of gold were found, expectations were not realized and investors shunned the colony.

NETHERLANDS INDIA

The twentieth century brought fabulous wealth to the Dutch East Indies. The subjugation of Achin Sultanate in northern Sumatra between 1898 and 1901 at length completed the conquest of the archipelago. Soil and climatic conditions were ideal for cultivating the tropical produce in world demand. Sugar output doubled between 1898 and 1913 (1.43 million tons in the latter year); tobacco yield doubled (163,000,000 pounds); tea exports quadrupled (53 million lbs.). Coffee growing, which suffered from plant disease, now yielded to other cultures and its production on Government estates was entirely abandoned. Rubber plantations were laid out after 1910 and quickly spread. Netherlands India likewise became a major oil producing area at this time, with output soaring from 90 to 480 million gallons. The Royal Dutch Petroleum Company, headed by Henri Deterding (1868-1939), was the chief operator and, after amalgamation in 1907 with the Shell Transport and Trading Company, a British concern, became a leading force in the industry. Tin mining, too, expanded rapidly. From 1898 to 1914, capital poured into the Dutch

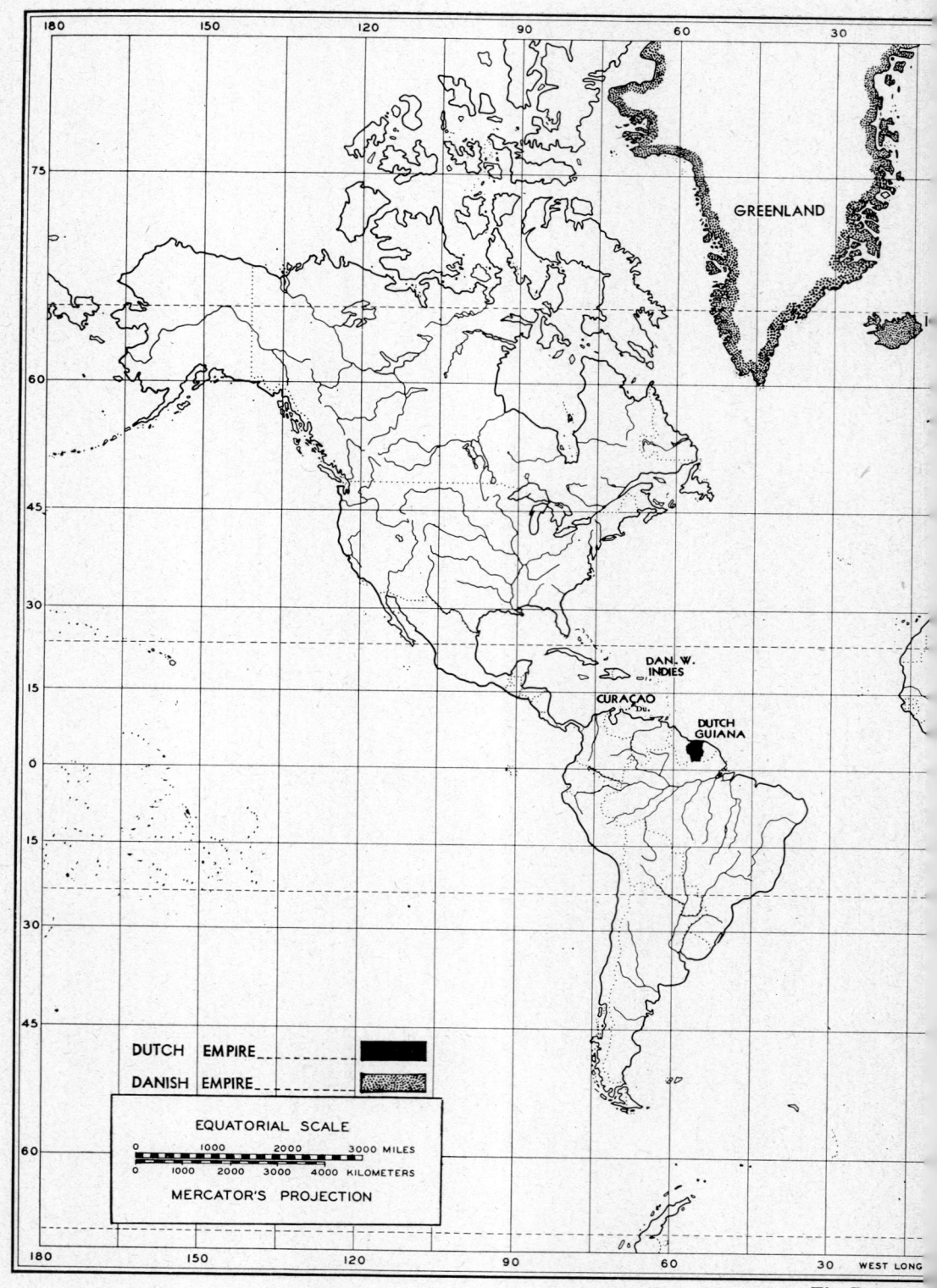

The Dutch a

THERLANDS

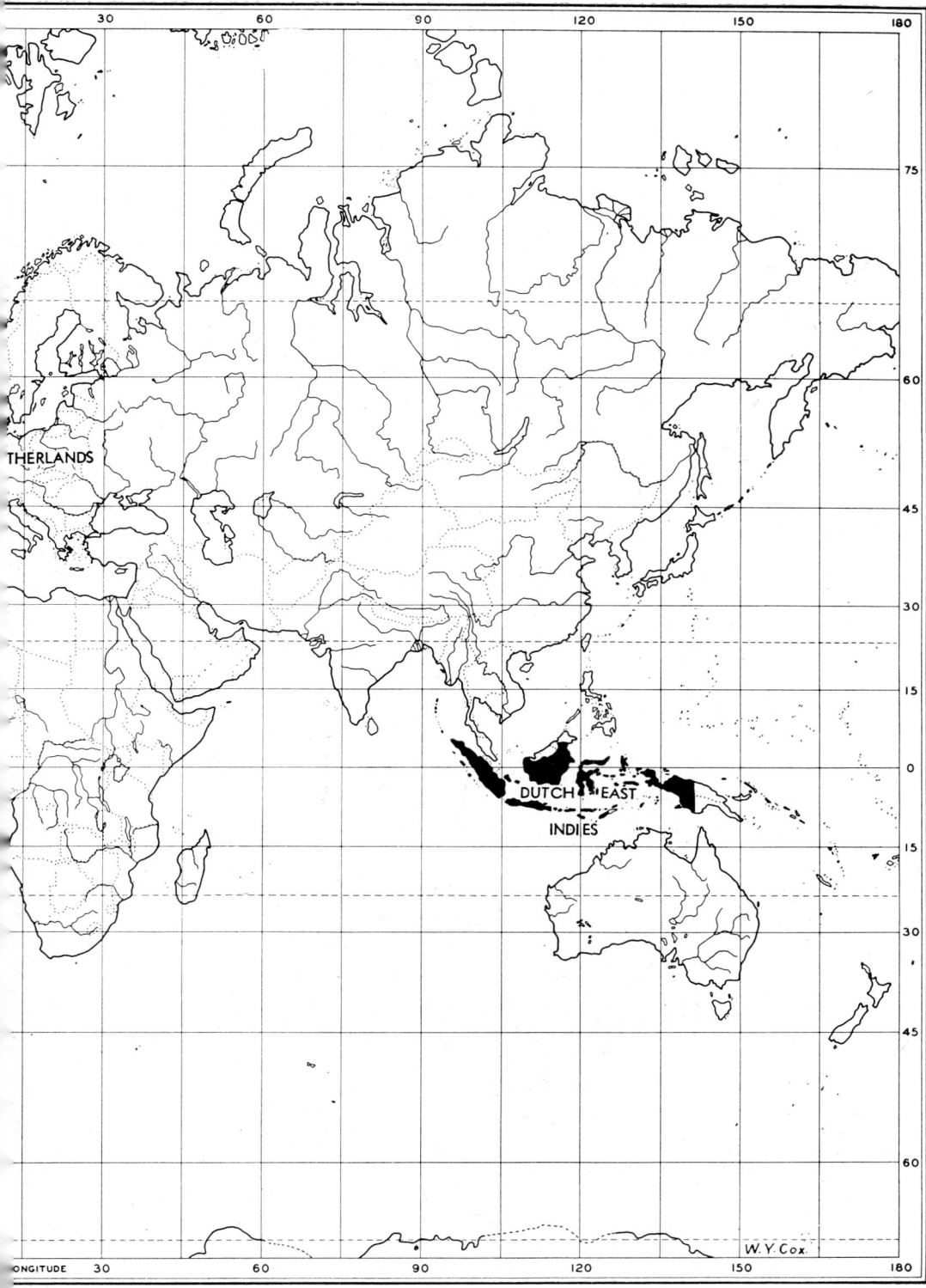

DUTCH EAST
INDIES

W. Y. Cox

ONGITUDE

ires in 1914

East Indies at an unprecedented rate, external commerce trebled (1.17 billion guilders in 1913) and huge fortunes emerged.

Boundless economic opportunity encouraged procreation and the population rose from 34 to 48 million in the fifteen years before the World War. Java now became one of the most densely peopled areas on the globe. Heavy Chinese immigration set in and by 1914 oriental competition was seriously embarrassing European business interests.

Native relations entered a new stage in 1905 when the Dutch Government began supervising the vassal princes' revenues to protect their subjects. Missionary work was actively fostered and the Christian element virtually doubled in the late 90's and early 1900's (600,000 in 1914). Forced labor was abolished in 1914. Natives were likewise encouraged to acquire land on hereditary lease. The number of schools and attendance trebled in this period—3,650 schools with 450,000 pupils were in operation by 1914. To avert discontents rooted in ambitions incapable of realization, instruction was of a practical nature and was conducted in native tongues.

The new century brought increasing demand for colonial participation in government. This was first met by the institution of local councils in 1903, some being composed of Europeans and natives and others of natives exclusively. Projects for an advisory Volksrad (People's Council) were formulated a decade later and such a body was ultimately established in 1916.

Despite Dutch Malaya's prosperity, there was commonly a deficit which the metropole covered by grants. This ranged from 2.5 million guilders at the turn of the century to 67.7 million in 1914. The colony's commerce and enterprises were, however, largely in Dutch hands and the burden was readily borne.

THE NETHERLANDS

Homeland indifference to colonies which followed abolition of the lucrative but iniquitous Culture System in 1870 gave way to lively interest and pride in empire about 1900. This change arose from the rapid development of the Dutch East Indies and affected all classes. Heavy investments were made; shipping, commerce and banking operations were kept chiefly in Dutch hands; and by 1914 East Indian profits played an important role in the metropole's financial life. Renewed interest in the overseas possessions found expression in serious efforts to ameliorate the natives' lot and allay colonial discontents, in fears respecting Japanese designs on the Indian archipelago and in attempts to revive the Caribbean possessions. By 1914 only the impotent Socialists sounded a discordant note—the Netherlanders as a whole were among the most ardently colonial-conscious peoples of Europe.

Chapter VIII

The Danish Empire
AMERICA

ICELAND

HOME rule, granted this dependency in 1874, failed to satisfy colonial aspirations. A constitutional amendment of 1909 provided for a Prime Minister who must be an islander but nationalist sentiment made rapid headway and led to general demand for independence. This was at length accorded in 1918 when Iceland became a separate kingdom with a common monarch, the sole remaining link between former colony and old metropole.

The introduction of motorboats early in the century profoundly influenced Iceland's economic development. Fishing now made rapid gains, large groups migrated from inland rural districts to the coast and emigration virtually ceased. New banking facilities (1904) eased credit and the organization of a marketing association (1911) fostered exports. Foreign trade consequently rose from 5.2 million kroner in 1900 to 15.5 million in 1914 and brought widespread prosperity to the community.

GREENLAND

The vogue for Arctic exploration from the 90's led to greatly increased knowledge respecting Greenland and to the mapping of most of its coastline by 1914. Foreign activity in this direction raised fears respecting territorial rights and, to forestall claims, Denmark's sovereignty was extended over the whole island in 1917.

Despite considerable agitation in Danish commercial circles, trade continued a state monopoly and the natives were carefully safeguarded against exploitation. Cryolite mining attained important proportions in the new century and raised the value of exports from 340,000 to 1,000,000 kroner between 1900 and 1914. The colony was, however, operated at a steady loss. Moravian missionaries who had opened work there in 1733 transferred their stations to the Danish Church in 1900, thus removing an important form of alien influence.

THE DANISH WEST INDIES

St. Croix, St. Thomas and St. John suffered progressive decline in the prewar years. Their external trade in 1900 was under 150,000 kroner—less than half of Greenland's. Soil exhaustion and shifted trade lanes precluded the possibility of recovery but their proximity to the Panama Canal gave them artificial value in American eyes. Negotiations for their purchase, which had opened in 1865 but which had failed because of senatorial opposition, were renewed by the United States at the turn of the century following disturbing rumors respecting German designs on the group. A treaty arranging for their transfer at $5,000,000 was signed in January 1902 and was ratified by the American Senate only to suffer rejection by the Danish Landsthing. Denmark, however, had no desire to continue a losing venture. The transaction was finally concluded in 1917 at the fantastic price of $25,000,000. The old metropole thus unexpectedly recovered all expenditures made in the islands' behalf and derived handsome profit from the venture—a unique episode in the annals of European expansion.

DENMARK *

The Danes had scant interest in overseas enterprise at this period. Icelandic discontent was viewed with friendly understanding and the grant of independence to the islanders was well received in the former mother country. Continuance in Greenland was regarded as a moral obligation. Failure to ratify the sale of the Caribbean possessions in 1902 arose from party conflict over domestic issues, a major one being the disposition of the sum involved, rather than from wounded pride over American rejection a generation earlier or from fear of losing prestige. No evidence of German pressure to block sale has been uncovered and ultimate conclusion of the transaction occasioned much satisfaction because of the large sum involved.

---

* The Faroe Islands, in the North Atlantic, are an integral part of Denmark.

Chapter IX

The Belgian Empire
THE BELGIAN CONGO

THE personal union existing between Belgium and the Congo Free State since the latter's creation in 1884 terminated in 1908 when this vast African state became a Belgian colony. Such action had been envisaged for many years.

In 1889 Leopold II (1835-1909), the common monarch, bequeathed his sovereign rights in the Congo to Belgium. Financial ties likewise drew the two countries together. The Free State had scant revenues and Leopold could not meet deficits from his private fortune. In 1890 he arranged for a loan from Belgium under which the kingdom received the option of annexing the Free State in 1901. This was not exercised but further loans followed.

In the interim the Free State Government claimed all vacant land and thus gained title to most of the area. Leopold took personal possession of an enormous tract and granted concessions in other districts to numerous trading concerns in which he held financial interest. Forced deliveries of ivory and rubber were imposed upon the natives and, when quotas fell short, terrorism was employed to stimulate effort. By 1900, the Free State had become a leading source of supply for both rubber and ivory but only through enslaving virtually the entire population. The episode formed one of the darkest chapters in African history.

Such iniquities could not long be veiled. By 1903 loud demands for reform were heard. Agitation centered in Great Britain and a report on Congo atrocities, by Roger Casement (1864-1916), the British consul at Boma, at length forced action. A commission of inquiry named by Leopold published its findings in 1905. These presented a damning indictment of the whole regime but no material changes followed. The British consequently annulled a lease on Soudanese territory (1906) affording the Free State an outlet on the Nile and threatened international action. To forestall the powers, the Belgian Government now reluctantly assumed control. A treaty of annexation insuring Leopold ample compensation was negotiated and the transfer took place on November 15, 1908. Belgium thus entered the ranks of

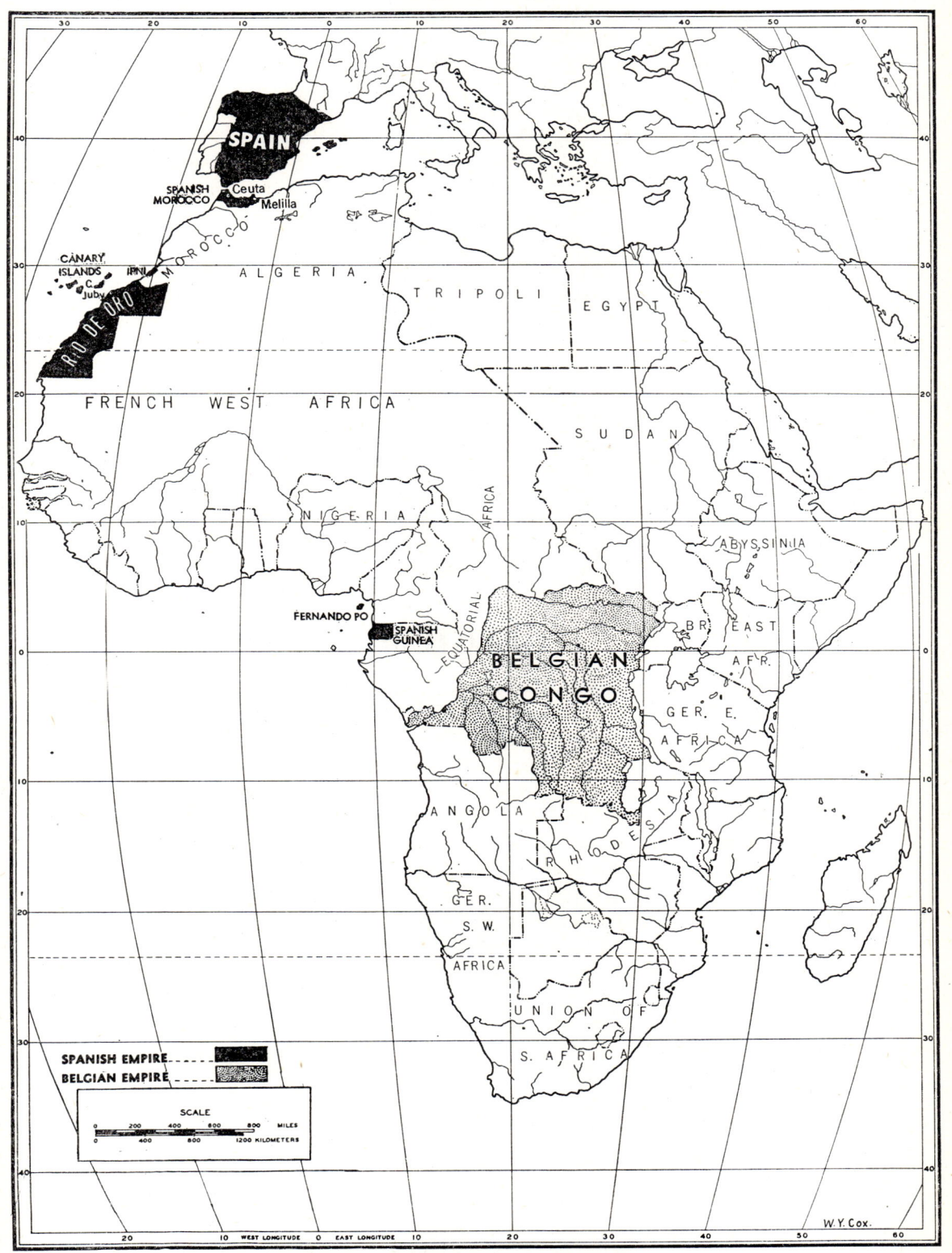

The Belguim and Spanish Empires in 1914

colonial powers under most unpropitious circumstances, the owner of a demoralized tropical dependency many times the parent state's size. Leopold's death a year later materially eased the situation.

Albert I (1875-1934) had visited the Congo on the eve of his accession and was keenly alive to its needs. Jules Renkin (1862-   ), the first Minister of Colonies, long a conscientious student of colonial affairs, surveyed the situation in person. A thorough overhauling of the entire structure followed. Land concessions were cancelled, deliveries of produce were abolished, missionary work was encouraged, free trade was instituted and the liquor traffic was curbed. While extensive use was made of native chiefs in administration, their activities were closely supervised. The new policy unhappily proved very costly; the deficit for 1914 exceeded 30 million francs. As a token of good will, the British Government ceded the western shore of Lake Albert to the Congo colony in 1910 and thus again gave it access to the Nile.

Belgian and foreign (largely British) capital now poured into the colony. Rubber and palm estates were laid out, gold and diamond beds were opened and methodical exploitation of the rich Katanga copper fields began. But development hinged on transportation. Rail construction was therefore inaugurated between the upper Congo and Lake Tanganyika, Rhodesia and Angola to provide outlets on the east, south and west. These lines were not opened until 1915, 1918 and 1931 respectively. Exports, which stood at 100 million francs in 1908, the last year under the old regime, consequently reached only 55 million in 1913. The deficit covered by the metropole rose as high as 20 million francs a year.

BELGIUM

Acquisition of the Congo evoked little enthusiasm at home. Its annexation was justified as a means of safeguarding loans to the Free State, of affording investment opportunities and of providing raw materials for industry as well as on grounds of moral responsibility. The facts that France held an option on the area from early Free State days and that Great Britain and Germany were obviously interested in it were used with telling effect. But conversion to imperialism proved difficult. In 1914 the Belgians as a whole still opposed the African adventure, holding that it was certain to embroil them in international rivalries, that Belgium could not afford the requisite army and navy, that colonization was entirely contrary to national tradition and that it would impose crushing financial burdens. Many freely advocated its sale before it be seized by some covetous power and Socialists habitually denounced the whole undertaking.

CHAPTER X

The Spanish Empire
AFTERMATH OF THE AMERICAN WAR

THE Spanish-American War cost Spain her status as an important colonial power. Sovereignty was relinquished over Cuba, and Puerto Rico, the Philippines and Guam were ceded to the United States (1899). The now isolated Ladrone (Marianne), Caroline and Pelew Islands in the North Pacific were sold to Germany in the same year. Three Moroccan ports (Ceuta, Melilla and Ifni), two strips of west African coastland (Rio de Oro and Rio Muni) and five Guinea Gulf islands (Fernando Po, Annobon, Elobey, Corisco and San Juan) were the only dependencies left this great pioneer in overseas expansion.[1] They offered scant economic opportunity and the exhausted metropole was in no position to develop them.

AFRICA

WESTERN SAHARA

A Franco-Spanish convention of 1900 set Rio de Oro's boundaries and accorded France the right of preemption over the territory should Spain ever decide to sell. Two later agreements, of 1904 and 1912, gave Spain the Cape Juby country to the north. The enlarged area was known as Western Sahara but it remained entirely unexploited and Spain had not yet occupied the newly-acquired district in 1914.

SPANISH GUINEA

Rio Muni and the adjacent islands were converted into the collective colony of Spanish Guinea, with Fernando Po as its administrative center, at the turn of the century. The Franco-Spanish convention of 1900 set Rio Muni's boundaries and accorded France an option on Guinea should the parent state at any time feel compelled to withdraw. Fernando Po's extraordinary fertility attracted British and

---
[1] The Canary Islands form an integral part of Spain.

German capitalists who opened numerous cacao plantations about 1910 with the aid of indentured mainland labor. Production was, however, still slight before the World War.

SPANISH MOROCCO

The disastrous American War dashed Spain's hopes of extending control over Morocco. Eminently practical, she now bent her energies to bringing at least a portion of the Sherifian Empire within her orbit. The international situation favored her purpose. Great Britain was unalterably opposed to the acquisition of territory opposite Gibraltar by another major European state but did not object to the presence of a minor power which could never menace her own position. France was not averse to Spanish control over the hinterland below Ceuta and Melilla if the rest of the country fell to her. The Entente Cordiale (1904) and a Franco-Spanish accord of the same year paved the way. In 1912, on the emergence of French Morocco, a Spanish protectorate was proclaimed over the northern portion of the old Empire save for Tangier which was internationalized because of its strategic position. Troops were moved in but anarchy reigned and control over the Spanish Zone continued purely nominal in 1914. Ifni, now an enclave in French Morocco, remained a Spanish possession under an agreement of 1912.

SPAIN

The events of 1898-1899 shattered Spain's prestige and destroyed Spanish morale. Efforts to restore both by developing the African possessions failed for lack of capital, and foreign investors, notably German, gained a paramount position in their economic life. One body of opinion consequently demanded the abandonment of all colonies as insupportable luxuries. Another called loudly for the acquisition of further lands as a means of rehabilitating national standing. The creation of Spanish Morocco was popularly hailed as marking the dawn of an era of regeneration. The protectorate consequently assumed symbolic value and expansion was again in public favor by 1914.

CHAPTER XI

The Russian Empire
THE FAR EAST

CONSTRUCTION of the Trans-Siberian Railroad east from Omsk after 1898 and its completion in 1906 precipitated a rush of pioneers into Siberia which profoundly altered the social and economic structure of that backward area. Now that communication and markets were assured, more than six million voluntary settlers crowded into the country under the lure of free homesteads and opened vast reaches of virgin soil. Forced colonization by criminals and religious dissenters was abolished in 1900 and only political prisoners were sent out thereafter. With mushroom settlements appearing on every hand, life attained the same fabulous proportions as in the American West a generation earlier. Siberia was definitely the Muscovite promised land, whose incredible resources lay almost untouched in 1914.

Russia now pressed down on China in an effort to secure a warm water outlet for Siberia. The Chinese Eastern Railway, running across Manchuria and affording a short cut from Vladivostok to the Trans-Siberian line, was built between 1896 and 1901 and opened this outlying Chinese province to Russian penetration. Conflict with Japan inevitably resulted. The Russian Government had not permitted the latter to annex the Liaotung Peninsula, off southern Manchuria, following her victory in the Sino-Japanese War of 1894-1895. In 1898 Russia herself secured a twenty-five year lease on much of the region together with the right to construct a railway through lower Manchuria from Port Arthur up to Harbin on the Chinese Eastern route. Acquisition of the entire area appeared imminent when Japan, which had vainly sought an understanding according her a foothold in Korea in return for recognizing Russia's position in Manchuria, suddenly called a halt by opening war in February 1904.

The Russo-Japanese War proved disastrous for Russia. Her troops were far removed from their base of supplies, her fighting machine collapsed and her Asiatic fleet was destroyed in August. Port Arthur was lost through siege the next January. A crushing defeat was suffered at Mukden in February. Three months later, her newly-arrived European fleet was annihilated in Tsushima Strait. The Revolution of 1905, which paralyzed the administration, made further resistance hopeless. The Japanese, on their side, were confronted by bankruptcy. A settlement was consequently negotiated at the instigation of President Theodore Roosevelt (1858-1919) who viewed Japan's emergence as a world power with apprehension. By the Treaty of Portsmouth (September 5, 1905), Russia yielded her lease and most of the Port Arthur-Harbin line to Japan, ceded the latter the lower half of Sakhalin Island which guarded the lower Amur valley, and accorded her a free hand in Korea.

While Russian expansion in the Far East was thus effectively checked, the tide of immigration into Siberia mounted steadily after the restoration of peace. Settlers poured in at the rate of three-quarters of a million a year and had established themselves throughout the entire area by the eve of the First World War.

THE MIDDLE EAST

Russian expansion in southwestern Asia now likewise brought on complications with Great Britain. Three spheres of rivalry developed—Thibet, Afghanistan and Persia (later Iran). Following rumors that a Romanov protectorate was in prospect, the British Government sent an expeditionary force into Thibet in 1903. This made its way to Lhasa, the capital, and, in September 1904, Lieutenant-Colonel Francis Younghusband (1863-   ) forced a treaty on Thibetan authorities whereby they pledged themselves not to alienate any territory to a third party, to exclude representatives of all foreign states save Britain and to grant no concessions without British consent. Russia was thus effectively checkmated.

In Afghanistan, the new Amir, Habibullah (1872-1919), who ascended the throne in 1901, firmly resisted British encroachments and appeared disposed to favor Russia as a counterbalance. Railway construction in adjacent Turkestan lent credence to reports that the Muscovites were seeking concessions at Kabul. At length in March 1905, great pressure by the British induced him to renew the protectorate established in the preceding reign. Two months later the British Government declared that it would regard any Russian attempt to penetrate Afghanistan by rail as an aggressive step. No more was heard of the matter and here, too, Russia's advance was halted.

She fared better in Iran. Economic infiltration through that country's northern provinces was well under way by 1900 and eyes were then turned to the Persian Gulf. Russian "explorers" and "physicians combatting plague" suddenly developed keen interest in the area. Greatly alarmed, the British Government announced in May 1903 that it would regard the establishment of a naval base on the Gulf by any other power as a menace to its own interests and would resist such action by all means at its disposal. Four years later British authorities proposed delimiting spheres of influence in Persia and the settlement of all outstanding territorial disputes as had been done with Russia's ally, France, in the Entente Cordiale of 1904. The Anglo-Russian Accord (August 1907) followed.

Iran was now split into three zones. The northern one (305,000 sq. m.) became a Russian sphere of influence; the southern one (137,000 sq. m.) fell within the British orbit; and the central one (188,000 sq. m.) continued subject to exploitation by both. Russia simultaneously disavowed designs on Afghanistan and the

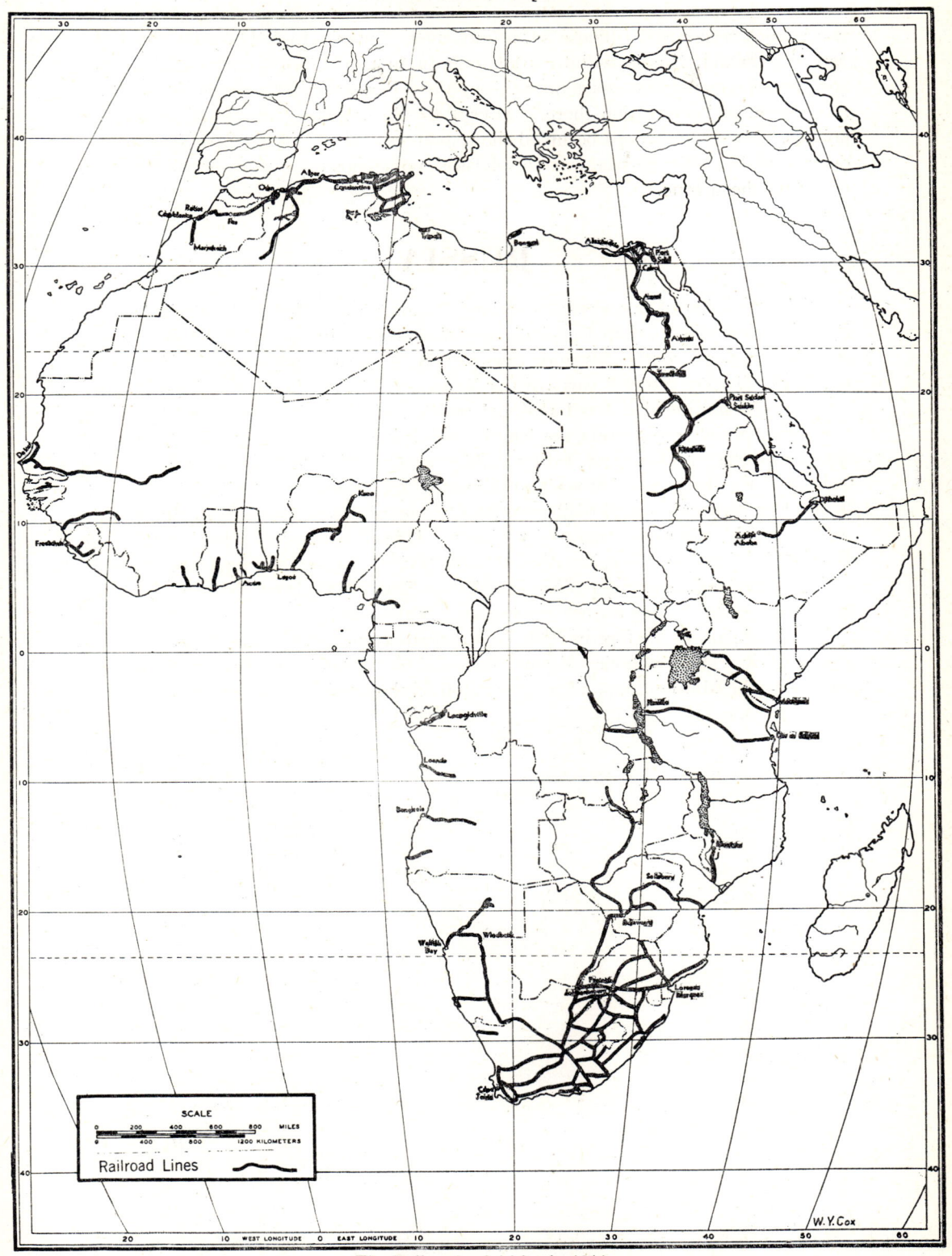

The Railroads of Africa in 1914

two parties recognized Chinese suzerainty over Thibet. In 1911 under the Potsdam Agreement, Russia withdrew her opposition to the Bagdad Railroad project and agreed to construct feeder lines through her Persian zone in return for German recognition of her position there. After 1907 she regularly interfered in Persian politics. Muscovite troops occupied the region west of the Caspian, settlers flocked down and by 1914 Russia was in physical possession of a considerable portion of the northern zone.

RUSSIA

The tradition of progressive overland expansion was deeply intrenched in the Russian mind and continued unchallenged throughout this period. All portions of the Empire were contiguous and, save for the spheres of influence in Manchuria and Iran, all were integral parts of the Romanov state. The acquisition of warm-water ports continued a fixed national policy and the sole difference of opinion respecting it centered around the lengths which might be pursued in attaining the desired objective. One party, led by A. M. Bezobrasov, the Secretary of State, who controlled Far Eastern relations, and Admiral Y. I. Alexeiev (1843-1904), Viceroy in the Far East, advocated deliberate provocation and war to eliminate Japan as a serious rival. Another, headed by Count Vladimir Lamsdorf (1845-1907), the Foreign Minister, and Sergius Witte (1849-1915), Minister of Finance, Commerce and Industry and directing genius of the Trans-Siberian Railroad, advocated caution and compromise. The former triumphed, Witte was dismissed and catastrophe followed. Again to the fore in 1906, Witte secured unexpectedly favorable terms at Portsmouth. The new policy of conciliation led to the Anglo-Russian understanding respecting the Middle East and concentration on the northern zone of Persia.

EUROPE
AFRICA
RUSSIA
RUSSIAN
TURKISH EMPIRE
PERSIA
AFGHANISTAN
INDI
Reval
Riga
Vilna
Warsaw
ST. PETERSBURG
MOSCOW
Nizhni Novgorod
Kief
Kharkof
Odessa
Saratof
Rostof
Tiflis
Baku
Tashkent
WEST LONGITUDE
EAST LONGITUDE
SCALE
0 500 1000 1500 MILES
0 500 1000 1500 2000 KILOMETERS
LAMBERT'S AZIMUTHAL EQUAL-AREA PROJECTION

The Ru

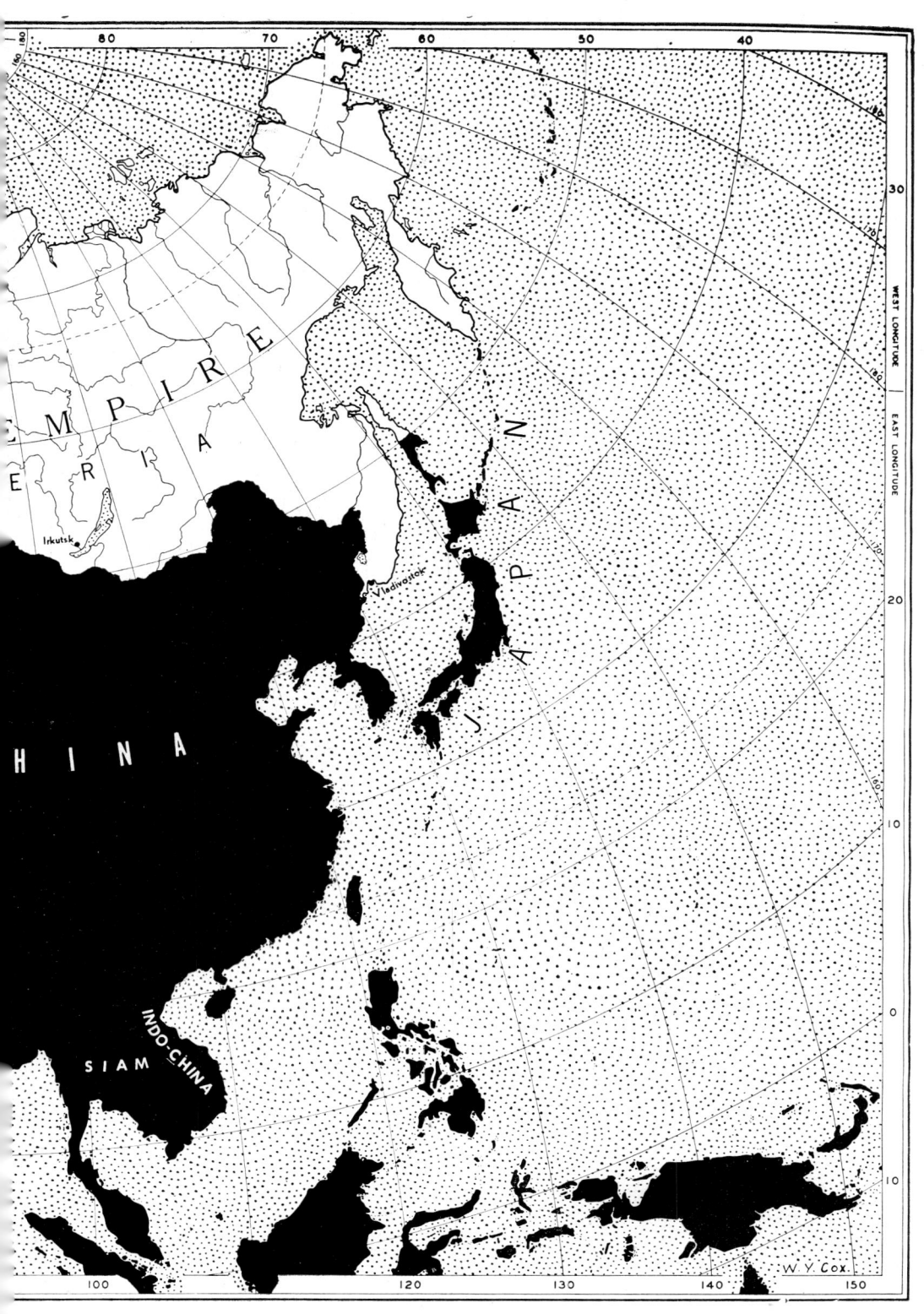

1914

Chapter XII

Trends in European Expansion, 1898-1914

TEMPERATE zone colonies had been the most highly-prized overseas possessions throughout the 1800's. Now, with the turn of the century, tropical dependencies assumed new importance. Unlimited demand for rubber, vegetable oils, cacao and fruit led investors to pour capital into such areas and interest came to center on them. Progress in tropical medicine—notably the conquest of yellow fever and advance in combatting sleeping sickness—improved living conditions in the hot countries and at length made residence there reasonably safe for whites.

An acute labor shortage followed the opening of mammoth plantations throughout the tropics. This led to grievous abuses which subjected the philosophy of "The White Man's Burden" to severe test. Inter-racial relations now entered a new stage. A mounting sense of responsibility towards the natives led to the opening of numerous schools but instruction was all too often of an impractical nature, creating social groups whose members scorned manual labor and became restive on failing to find outlets for their talents as members of the white-collared class.

Nationalist movements made rapid headway and challenged white supremacy. Japan's defeat of Russia, shattering European prestige, inspired subject peoples throughout the world to assert themselves against their masters. The small voice in government accorded the natives failed to appease them and by 1914 western imperialism stood definitely on the defensive.

Spheres of influence, which had given way to protectorates and colonies throughout Africa, now reappeared in Asia. Small colonies were merged to form large ones. A marked extension of colonial rights occurred. Rapid progress of the dominion movement served to integrate the British Empire. The extension of protective tariffs led to intra-empire preference. Mounting trade restrictions abroad gave colonies added value both as markets and as sources of supply. Pride in empire, characterizing nationalism in the new century, had its roots in economic factors.

Overseas rivalries now played an increasingly important role in shaping international relations. Anglo-German tension after 1890 rested largely on colonial disputes and competition in foreign markets. These extra-European clashes led to the Entente Cordiale (1904) between Great Britain and France—a diplomatic revolution of unparalleled significance. The Anglo-Japanese alliance of 1902 arose through mutual hostility for Russia based on conflicting territorial ambitions. Cordial feelings between Great Britain and Russia were reestablished by the adjustment of such disputes under the Convention of 1907. The Anglo-German rapprochement of 1913-1914 took shape along similar lines.

Franco-German animosity, which became a dominant factor in world affairs after 1905, was kept at fever heat by the Moroccan Question. This led to the Algeciras Conference (1906), the first important gathering of the powers in the new century. The partitioning of North Africa early in the century tightened bonds between the Latin states of Europe—France, Spain and Italy. As never before, colonies formed pawns on the chessboard of international politics. The complex diplomatic history of Europe from Fashoda to the First World War can be understood only in the light of imperialistic rivalries marking those years.

The migration of European capital overseas now attained unprecedented proportions. British, German and French investments in colonial ventures were especially heavy and were frequently made beyond the jurisdiction of the national flag. The resultant economic interdependence served to restrain conflict abroad and operated powerfully in the interests of peace.

The pre-war missionary differed widely from his nineteenth century predecessor. He placed less emphasis upon religion and more upon social welfare. A new spirit of tolerance was accompanied by a keen interest in native languages and institutions. Veritable African, Oriental and South Sea cults emerged and attained wide followings in the colonizing countries of Europe during the early 1900's. This interesting development coincided with a new critical attitude towards occidental civilization among subject peoples in general and a sharp reversion to indigenous cultures.

Westernization of the world, which had proceeded apace since early modern times, was now, for the first time, subjected to challenge. The most conspicuous setback occurred in the religious sphere. Natives had, quite generally, come to view Christianity as an instrument of subjection and by 1914 antipathy for the alien faith of their masters was turning into open hostility. This was but one of many signs affording incontestable evidence that European expansion had reached its apogee early in the century. Imperialism was about to kick back and on the eve of the First World War the days of European domination in Africa, Asia and Oceania were already clearly numbered.

SELECT BIBLIOGRAPHY

THE BACKGROUND

J. L. Barton. *The Missionary and His Critics.* New York, 1906.
M. J. Bonn. *Nationale Kolonialpolitik.* Munich, 1910.
H. Friedjung. *Das Zeitalter des Imperialismus, 1884-1914.* 3 vols., Berlin, 1919-1920.
H. A. Gibbons. *The New Map of Africa, 1900-1916.* New York, 1916.
———. *The New Map of Asia, 1900-1919.* New York, 1919.
Karl Kautsky. *Sozialismus und Kolonialpolitik.* Berlin, 1907.
Gustav Noske. *Colonial Policy and Social Democracy.* London, 1914.
E. J. Payne. *Colonies and Colonial Federation.* London, 1905.
Paul Reinsch. *Colonial Administration.* New York, 1905.
J. W. Root. *Colonial Tariffs.* Liverpool, 1906.
A. H. Snow. *The Administration of Dependencies.* New York, 1902.
Armin Vámbéry. *Western Culture in Eastern Lands.* London, 1906.
R. D. Ward. "Some Problems of the Tropics," in *Bulletin of the American Geographical Society*, January 1908, pp. 7 ff.

THE BELGIAN COLONIAL EMPIRE

G. K. Anton. *Kongostaat und Kongoreform.* Leipzig, 1911.
Jean Bertrand. *Le Congo Belge.* Brussels, 1909.
Louis Bertrand. *Le Scandale Congolais.* Brussels, 1908.
Joseph Blanc. *Le Droit de Préférence de la France sur le Congo Belge, 1884-1911.* Paris, 1921.
Francesco Bottaro-Costa. *Congo: Problemi di Politica Coloniale Belga.* Rome, 1912.
H. R. F. Bourne. *Civilization in Congoland.* London, 1903.
Roger Brunet. *L'Annexion du Congo à la Belgique et le Droit International.* Paris, 1911.
M. Calmeyn. *Au Congo Belge.* Paris, 1912.
A. Castelein. *The Congo State.* London, 1907.
F. Cattier. *Droit et Administration de l'Etat Indépendant du Congo.* Brussels, 1898.
———. *Etude sur la Situation de l'Etat Indépendant du Congo.* Brussels, 1906.
Alphonse de Haulleville. *Les Aptitudes Colonisatrices des Belges et la Question Coloniale en Belgique.* Brussels, 1898.
Charles de Lannoy. *L'Organisation Coloniale Belge.* Brussels, 1913.
Lieutenant-General Donny. "Les Relations du Congo Belge avec la Mère Patrie," in *Bulletin de la Société Royale Belge d'Etudes Coloniales*, 1912, pp. 805 ff.
René Dubreucq. *A Travers le Congo Belge.* Brussels, 1909.
A. Goffart and G. Morissens. *Le Congo.* Brussels, 1908.
F. Goffart. "Les Concessions Caoutchoutières du Bassin du Congo," in *Revue Générale*, August 1908, pp. 235 ff.
———. *L'Outillage Economique et la Mise en Valeur du Congo Belge.* Brussels, 1913.
———. *La Valeur et l'Avenir Economique du Congo Belge.* Louvain, 1912.
W. C. Hill. *Select Bibliography of Publications on Foreign Colonisation ... Belgian (etc.) ....* London, 1915.
V. Jentgen. *La Terre Belge du Congo.* Brussels, 1911.

Louis Jozon. *L'Etat Indépendant du Congo.* Paris, 1900.
Victor Levy. *Im belgischen Congostaate.* Vienna, 1901.
O. Louwers. *Eléments du Droit de l'Etat Indépendant du Congo.* Brussels, 1907.
Louis Navez. *Essai Historique sur l'Etat Indépendant du Congo.* Brussels, 1905.
Ernest Nys. "Le Droit de Préférence de la France," in *Le Mouvement Géographique,* July 30, 1911, pp. 379 ff.
Egide Pâque. *Notre Colonie: Etude Pratique sur le Congo Belge.* Namur, 1910.
Unsigned. "Railroads in the Congo Free State," in *Bulletin of the American Geographical Society,* August 1907, pp. 482 ff.
Emile Vandervelde. *La Belgique et le Congo.* Paris, 1911.
—————. *Les Derniers Jours de l'Etat Indépendant du Congo.* Brussels, 1909.
René Vauthier. *Le Congo Belge.* Brussels, 1910.
A. S. J. Vermeersch. *La Question Congolese.* Brussels, 1906.
—————. *Les Destinées du Congo Belge.* Brussels, 1907.
H. Waltz. *Das Konzessionswesen im belgischen Kongo.* 2 vols., Jena, 1917.
A. J. Wauters. "La Colonisation Belge au Congo et l'Initiative Privée," in *Le Mouvement Géographique,* January 7, 1912, pp. 1 ff.
—————. *L'Etat Indépendant du Congo.* Brussels, 1899
—————. *Histoire Politique du Congo Belge.* Brussels, 1911.
M. Wilmotte. "La Belgique et l'Etat Indépendant du Congo," in *Revue de Paris,* May 1, 1902, p. 146.

THE BRITISH COLONIAL EMPIRE

GENERAL

W. J. Ashley, ed. *The British Dominions: Their Present Commercial and Industrial Condition.* London, 1911.
Emile Baillaud. *La Politique Indigène de l'Angleterre en Afrique Occidentale.* Paris, 1912.
C. E. A. Bedwell, ed. *The Legislation of the Empire: Being a Survey of the Legislative Enactments of the British Dominions from 1898 to 1907.* 4 vols., London, 1909.
Victor Bérard. *British Imperialism and Commercial Supremacy.* London, 1906.
C. W. Boyd, ed. *Mr. Chamberlain's Speeches.* 2 vols., London, 1914.
C. Bright. *Imperial Telegraphic Communication.* London, 1911.
Joseph Chamberlain. *Imperial Union and Tariff Reform.* London, 1903.
Lionel Curtis. *The Problem of the Commonwealth.* London, 1916.
J. Davidson. *Commercial Federation and Colonial Trade Policy.* London, 1900.
R. M. Dawson, ed. *The Development of Dominion Status, 1900-1936.* Oxford, 1937.
Geoffrey Drage. *The Imperial Organization of Trade.* London, 1911.
J. G. Findlay. *The Imperial Conference of 1911 from Within.* London, 1912.
J. F. C. Fuller. *Imperial Defence, 1588-1914.* London, 1926.
A. J. Herbertson and O. J. R. Howarth, eds. *The Oxford Survey of the British Empire.* 6 vols., Oxford, 1914.
Richard Jebb. *The Britannic Question: A Survey of Alternatives [Alliance As Equal States vs. Imperial Federation].* London, 1913.
—————. *The Imperial Conference.* 2 vols., London, 1911.
—————. *Studies in Colonial Nationalism.* London, 1905.
S. H. Jeyes. *Mr. Chamberlain.* New York, 1903.
H. H. Johnston. *The British Empire in Africa.* London, 1910.
A. B. Keith. *Imperial Unity and the Dominions.* Oxford, 1916.
A. L. Lowell and H. M. Stephens. *Colonial Civil Service ... in England, Holland and France.* New York, 1900.
C. P. Lucas. *The British Empire.* London, 1915.
Alexander Mackintosh. *Joseph Chamberlain.* London, 1914.
Charles Petrie. *Joseph Chamberlain.* London, 1940.
A. F. Pollard, ed. *The British Empire.* London, 1909.
J. W. Root. *The Trade Relations of the British Empire.* Liverpool, 1904.
E. Sanderson. *Great Britain in Modern Africa.* London, 1907.
A. J. Sargent. *The Sea Road to the East: Gibraltar to Wei-Hai-Wei.* London, 1912.
A. B. Silburn. *Colonies and Imperial Defense.* London, 1909.
C. H. Stigand. *Administration in Tropical Africa.* London, 1914.
C. E. T. Stuart-Linton. *Problems of Empire Governance.* London, 1912.

N. W. Thomas, ed. *Native Races of the British Empire.* 4 vols., London, 1906-1907.
Unsigned. "England and Russia in Central Asia," in *Journal of the American Asiatic Association,* March 1909, pp. 42 ff.
G. M. Wrong. "The Growth of Nationalism in the British Empire," in *The American Historical Review,* October 1916, pp. 45 ff.

ADEN

R. R. Robbins. "The Legal Status of Aden Colony and the Aden Protectorate," in *The American Journal of International Law,* October 1939, pp. 700 ff.
H. G. C. Swayne. "The Rock of Aden," in *The National Geographic Magazine,* December 1935, pp. 723 ff.

AUSTRALIA

C. D. Allin. *The Early Federation Movement of Australia.* Kingston, 1907.
J. G. Bartholomew and K. R. Cramp. *Australasian School Atlas.* Edinburgh, 1915.
Thomas Bateson. *A Short History of Australia.* London, 1911.
W. G. Beach. "The Australian Federal Constitution," in *The Political Science Quarterly,* December 1899, pp. 663 ff.
A. I. Clark. *Studies in Australian Constitutional Law.* Melbourne, 1901.
V. S. Clark. *The Labor Movement in Australasia: A Study in Social Democracy.* London, 1907.
T. A. Coghlan and T. T. Ewing. *The Progress of Australasia in the Nineteenth Century.* London, 1902.
Brian Fitzpatrick. *The British Empire in Australia: An Economic History, 1834-1939.* Melbourne, 1941.
H. E. Gregory. "Lonely Australia: The Unique Continent," in *The National Geographic Magazine,* December 1916, pp. 473 ff.
J. W. Gregory. *Australia.* Cambridge, 1916.
J. G. Grey. *Australasia Old and New.* London, 1901.
W. H. Lang. *Australia.* London, 1908.
H. H. Lusk. "The Australian Commonwealth," in *The Journal of School Geography,* March 1901, pp. 90 ff.
Henri Merens. *Etude sur les Colonies Anglaises Autonomes de l'Australie et du Canada.* Toulouse, 1907.
Albert Métin. *La Socialisme sans Doctrines: La Question Agraire et la Question Ouvrière en Australie et Nouvelle-Zélande.* Paris, 1910.
W. H. Moore. *The Constitution of the Commonwealth of Australia.* Melbourne, 1910.
John Quick and R. R. Garran, eds. *Annotated Constitution of the Australian Commonwealth.* Sydney, 1901.
J. D. Rogers. *Australasia.* Oxford, 1907.
A. J. J. St. Ledger. *Australian Socialism.* London, 1909.
Baldwin Spencer and F. J. Gillen. *Native Tribes of the Northern Territory of Australia.* London, 1914.
——————. *The Northern Tribes of Central Australia.* London, 1904.
J. T. Sutcliffe. *A History of Trade Unionism in Australia.* Melbourne, 1921.
A. W. Tilby. *Australasia, 1688-1911.* London, 1912.
H .G. Turner. *The First Decade of the Australian Commonwealth.* London, 1911.
Unsigned. "Transcontinental Railroads in Australia," in *Bulletin of the American Geographical Society,* December 1902, pp. 410 ff.
Eugene van Cleef. "Climatic Influences in the Economic Development of Australia," in *Bulletin of the Geographical Society of Philadelphia,* October 1910, pp. 1 ff.
B. R. Wise. *The Commonwealth of Australia.* London, 1913.

BERMUDA AND THE CARIBBEAN ISLANDS

A. E. Aspinall. *The British West Indies.* London, 1913.
W. B. Hayward. *Bermuda Past and Present.* London, 1933.
C. H. Hull. "Finances in the British West Indies," in American Economic Association, *Essays in Colonial Finance.* New York, 1900, pp. 168 ff.
J. W. Root. *The British West Indies and the Sugar Industry.* Liverpool, 1899.
Eugène Sicé. *Comment Gouverner les Colonies Tropicales: Etude sur le Gouvernement Local et l'Organisation Législative des Antilles Anglaises.* Paris, 1913.

BRITISH EAST AFRICA

Emile Baillaud. *La Politique Indigène de l'Angleterre en Afrique Orientale.* Paris, 1912.
Gustavo Chiesi. *La Colonizzazione Europea nell'Est Africa: Italia-Inghilterra-Germania.* Turin, 1909.
C. N. Eliot. *The East African Protectorate.* London, 1905.
A. R. Tucker. *Eighteen Years in Uganda and East Africa.* London, 1911.

BRITISH MALAYA

S. Baring-Gould and C. A. Bampfylde. *A History of Sarawak Under its Two White Rajahs, 1839-1908.* London, 1909.
Charles Bruce. *Twenty Years in Borneo.* London, 1924.
Oscar Cook. *Borneo.* London, 1924.
W. A. Graham. *Kelantan.* Glasgow, 1908.
J. M. Hubbard. "Colonial Government in Sarawak in Borneo," in *The National Geographic Magazine,* September 1900, pp. 359 ff.
Walter Makepeace, ed. *One Hundred Years of Singapore.* 2 vols., London, 1921.
W. G. Maxwell and W. S. Gibson, eds. *Treaties and Engagements Affecting the Malay States and Borneo.* London, 1924.
Owen Rutter. *British North Borneo.* London, 1922.
W. W. Skeat and C. O. Blagden. *Pagan Races of the Malay Peninsula.* 2 vols., London, 1906.
A. R. Wallace. *The Malay Archipelago.* London, 1898.
A. B. Ward. *Outlines of Sarawak History, 1839-1917.* Kuching, 1927.
R. O. Winstedt. *A History of Perak.* Singapore, 1934.
——————. *Malaya, the Straits Settlements and the Federated and Unfederated Malay States.* London, 1923.
Arnold Wright. *Twentieth Century Impressions of British Malaya.* London, 1908.
Arnold Wright and T. H. Reid. *The Malay Peninsula.* London, 1912.

BRITISH SOMALILAND

H. R. F. Bourne. *The Story of Somaliland.* London, 1904.
Great Britain. War Office. *Précis of Information Concerning Somaliland.* 2 vols., London, 1902.
J. A. Hamilton. *Somaliland.* London, 1911.

CANADA

A. L. Bishop. "The Development of Wheat Production in Canada," in *Bulletin of the American Geographical Society,* January 1912, pp. 10 ff.
A. G. Bradley. *Canada in the Twentieth Century.* Westminster, 1903.
George Bryce. *Canadian Loyalty.* Winnipeg, 1902.
——————. *A History of Manitoba.* Toronto, 1906.
W. H. P. Clement. *The Law of the Canadian Constitution.* London, 1915.
L. E. Ellis. *Reciprocity, 1911: A Study in Canadian-American Relations.* New Haven, 1939.
Robert England. *The Colonization of Western Canada, 1896-1934.* London, 1936.
J. B. Hedges. *Building the Canadian West.* New York, 1939.
——————. *The Federal Railway Land Subsidy Policy of Canada.* Cambridge, 1934.
H. A. Innes. *A History of the Canadian Pacific Railway.* London, 1923.
M. Q. Innis. *An Economic History of Canada.* Toronto, 1935.
A. H. Lefroy. *Canada's Federal System.* Toronto, 1913.
Edward Porritt. *The Revolt in Canada Against the New Feudalism: Tariff History from the Revision of 1907 to the Uprising of the West in 1910.* London, 1911.
——————. *Sixty Years of Protection in Canada, 1846-1907.* London, 1908.
Louis Riou. "La Liberté Commerciale et les Idées Economiques au Canada," in *Revue Trimestrielle Canadienne,* August 1915, pp. 171 ff.
Adam Shortt and Arthur Doughty, eds. *Canada and Its Provinces: A History of the Canadian People and Their Institutions.* 23 vols., Toronto, 1914.
André Siegfried. *The Race Question in Canada.* London, 1907.
F. A. Talbot. "Economic Prospects of . . . British Columbia," in *Bulletin of the American Geographical Society,* March 1912, pp. 167 ff.
J. van Sommer. *Canada and the Empire.* Toronto, 1898.
A. S. Whiteley. "The Peopling of the Prairie Provinces of Canada," in *The American Journal of Sociology,* September 1932, pp. 240 ff.

CEYLON

W. A. Clark. "The Commerce of Ceylon," in *Journal of the American Asiatic Association,* October 1907, pp. 274 ff.
René Delaporte. *Ceylan.* Paris, 1913.
W. C. Magelssen. "The Trade and Industries of Ceylon," in *Journal of the American Asiatic Association,* February 1912, pp. 16 ff.
H. S. Smith. "The Pearl Fisheries of Ceylon," in *The National Geographic Magazine,* February 1912, pp. 173 ff.

EGYPT AND THE SOUDAN

H. R. F. Bourne. *Egypt Under British Control.* London, 1906.
Auckland Colvin. *The Making of Modern Egypt.* London, 1909.
Lord Cromer. *Modern Egypt.* 2 vols., New York, 1908.
C. de Freycinet. *La Question d'Egypte.* Paris, 1904.
M. H. Haekal. *La Dette Publique Egyptienne.* Paris, 1912.
Sidney Low. *Egypt in Transition.* London, 1914.
J. J. Mathews. *Egypt and the Formation of the Anglo-French Entente of 1904.* Philadelphia. 1939.
G. Pemeant. *L'Egypte et la Politique Française.* Paris, 1909.
L. J. Ragatz. *The Question of Egypt in Anglo-French Relations, 1875-1904.* Edinburgh, 1922.
M. von Hagen. *England und Aegypten.* Bonn, 1915.

THE FALKLAND ISLANDS

V. F. Boyson. *The Falkland Islands.* Oxford, 1924.
C. F. Jones. "The Economic Activities of the Falkland Islands," in *The Geographical Review,* July 1924, pp. 394 ff.

GAMBIA

F. B. Archer. *The Gambia Colony and Protectorate.* London, 1910.
H. F. Reeve. *Gambia.* London, 1912.

GOLD COAST

W. W. Claridge. *A History of the Gold Coast and Ashanti.* 2 vols., London, 1915.
George Macdonald. *The Gold Coast, Past and Present.* London, 1898.

HONG KONG

G. E. Anderson. "The Commerce of Hong Kong," in *Journal of the American Asiatic Association,* September 1911, pp. 243 ff.
──────. "The Foreign Commerce of Hong Kong," in *Journal of the American Asiatic Association,* July 1913, pp. 179 ff.
Geoffrey Sayer. *Hong Kong.* New York, 1937.
A. P. Wilder. "The Commerce of Hong Kong," in *Journal of the American Asiatic Association,* August 1907, pp. 206 ff.

INDIA

J. D. Anderson. *The Peoples of India.* Cambridge, 1913.
B. H. Baden-Powell and T. W. Holderness. *A Short Account of the Land Revenue and Its Administration in British India.* London, 1913.
E. R. Bevan. *Indian Nationalism.* London, 1913.
Sudhindra Bose. *Some Aspects of British Rule in India.* Iowa City, 1916.
Joseph Chailley-Bert. *Administrative Problems in British India.* London, 1910.
Alfred Chatterton. *Agricultural and Industrial Problems in India.* Madras, 1912.
──────. *Industrial Evolution in India.* Madras, 1912.
Valentine Chirol. *Indian Unrest.* London, 1910.
W. A. Clark. "Modern India," in *Journal of the American Asiatic Association,* November 1907, pp. 307 ff.
Harold Clayton. *Rural Development in Burma.* Rangoon, 1911.
Henry Cotton. *New India: Or, India in Transition.* London, 1907.
──────. "The New Spirit in India," in *Journal of the American Asiatic Association,* December 1906, pp. 341 ff.
William Crooke. *Natives of Northern India.* Calcutta, 1907.

J. Dautremer. *Burma Under British Rule.* London, 1913.
M. de P. Webb. *India and the Empire: A Consideration of the Tariff Problem.* London, 1908.
James Douie. *The Punjab, Northwest Frontier Province and Kashmir.* Cambridge, 1916.
Romesh Dutt. *Famines and Land Assessments in India.* London, 1900.
L. Fraser. *India Under Curzon and After.* London, 1911.
J. B. Fuller. *The Empire of India.* London, 1913.
T. W. Holderness. *Peoples and Problems of India.* New York, 1912.
Thomas Holdich. *India.* London, 1904.
Alleyne Ireland. *The Province of Burma: Colonial Administration in the Far East.* 2 vols., New York, 1907.
A. C. Lovett and G. F. MacMunn. *The Armies of India.* London, 1911.
Albert Métin. *L'Inde d'Aujourd'hui: Etude Sociale.* Paris, 1903.
Mary Minto, ed. *India: Minto and Morley, 1905-1910.* New York, 1934.
D. N. Mitter. *The Position of Women in Hindu Law.* Calcutta, 1913.
Theodore Morison. *The Economic Transition in India.* London, 1911.
Viscount Morley. *Indian Speeches, 1907-1909.* London, 1909.
R. Mukerjee. *The Foundations of Indian Economics.* London, 1916.
J. B. Pratt. *India and Its Faiths.* Boston, 1915.
Julius Richter. *A History of Missions in India.* Edinburgh, 1908.
H. H. Risley. *The People of India.* London, 1915.
H. B. L. Smith. *India and the Tariff Problem.* London, 1909.
John Strachey. *India: Its Administration and Progress.* London, 1911.
Unsigned. "The Population of India," in *Bulletin of the American Geographical Society,* July 1904, pp. 408 ff.
W. L. Warner. *The Native States of India.* London, 1910.
William Wedderburn. *Allan Octavian Hume: Father of the Indian National Congress.* London, 1913.

THE MEDITERRANEAN "LIFE-LINE"

W. C. Abbott. *An Introduction to the Documents Relating to the International Status of Gibraltar, 1704-1934.* New York, 1935.
René Delaporte. *L'Ile de Chypre.* Paris, 1913.
G. T. Garratt. *Gibraltar and the Mediterranean.* New York, 1939.
C. W. J. Orr. *Cyprus Under British Rule.* London, 1918.
N. Slousch. "Malte: Ses Habitants et leur Langue," in *Revue du Monde Musulman,* August 1908, pp. 631 ff.

NEWFOUNDLAND

J. D. Rogers. *Newfoundland.* Oxford, 1911.
C. M. Skinner. "The Railway in Newfoundland," in *Bulletin of the American Geographical Society,* November 1905, pp. 658 ff.
F. E. Smith. *The Story of Newfoundland.* London, 1920.

NEW ZEALAND

James Cowan. *The Maori of New Zealand.* Christchurch, 1910.
A. P. Douglas. *The Dominion of New Zealand.* London, 1909.
J. W. Gregory. *Australia and New Zealand.* London, 1907.
James Hight and H. D. Bamford. *The Constitutional History and Law of New Zealand.* Christchurch, 1914.
J. E. le Rossignol and W. D. Stewart. *State Socialism in New Zealand.* New York, 1910.
P. Marshall. "The Commercial Geography of New Zealand," in *Bulletin of the Geographical Society of Philadelphia,* January 1910, pp. 17 ff.
Henri Merens. *Etude sur les Colonies Anglaises Autonomes de l'Australie et du Canada.* Toulouse, 1907.
Albert Métin. *La Socialisme sans Doctrines: La Question Agraire et la Question Ouvrière en Australie et Nouvelle-Zélande.* Paris, 1910.
G. H. Scholefield. *New Zealand in Evolution.* London, 1916.
André Siegfried. *Democracy in New Zealand.* London, 1914.
Unsigned. "The Maoris of New Zealand," in *The National Geographic Magazine,* March 1907, pp. 198 ff.

The Rai

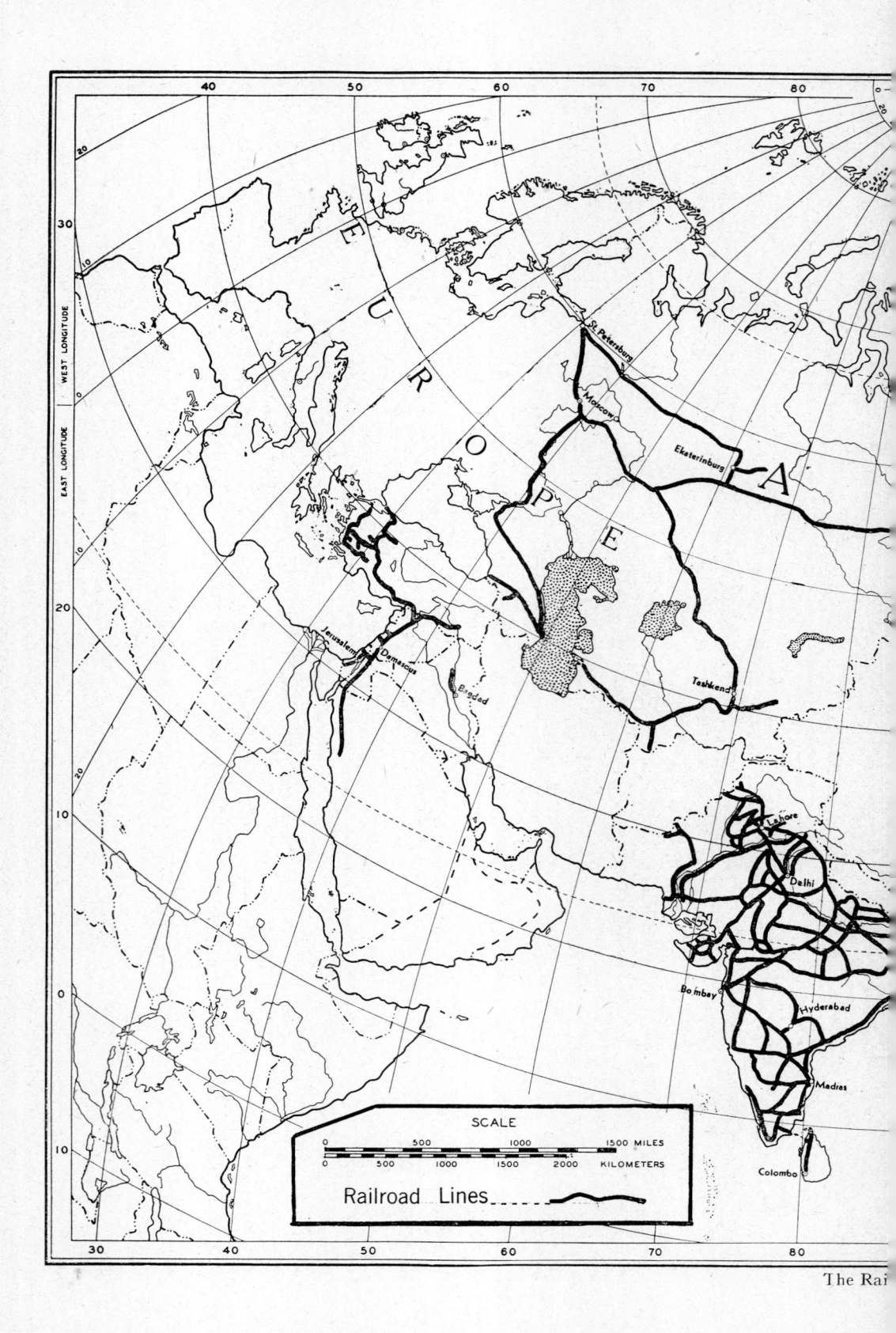

in 1914

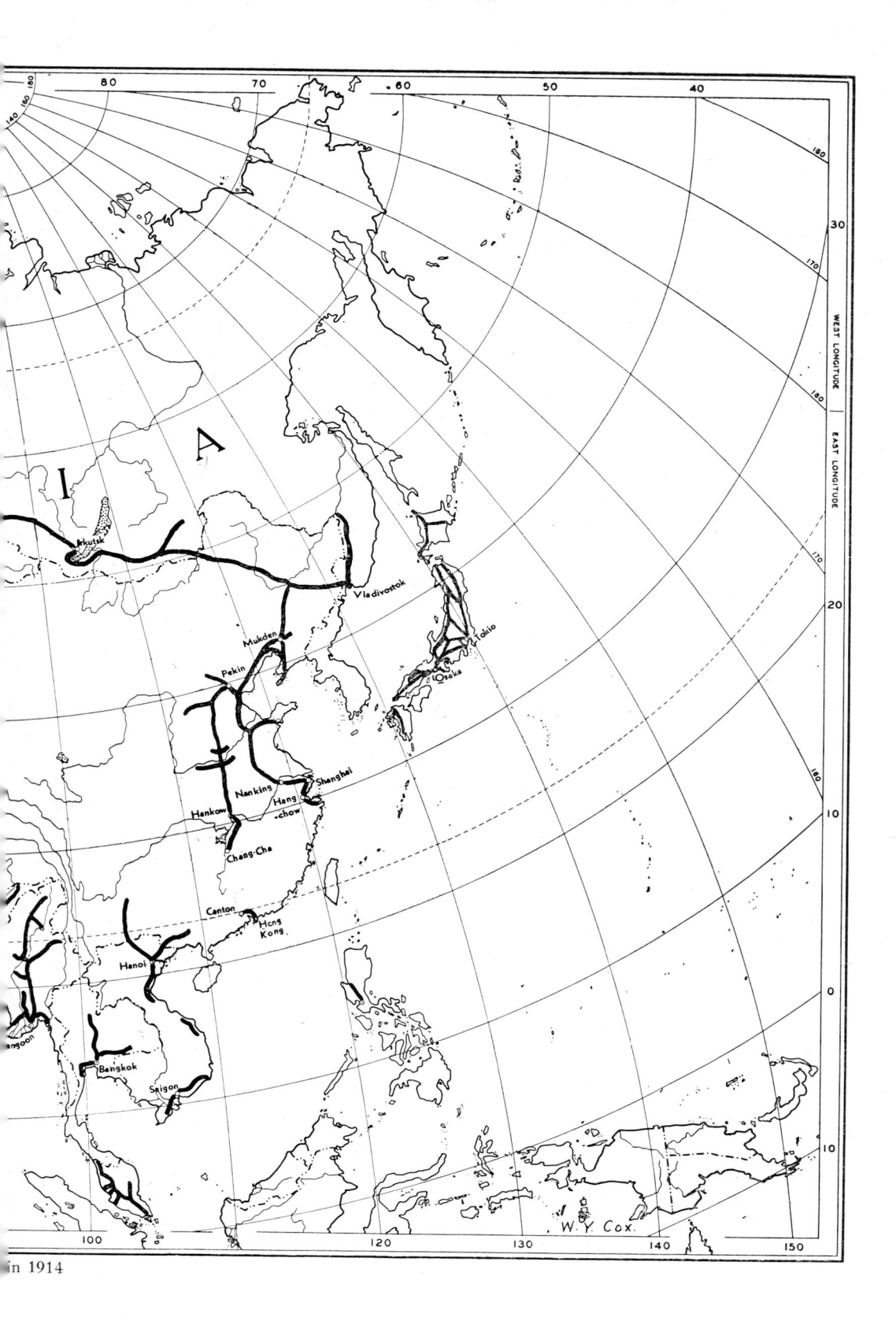

NIGERIA

A. F. Calvert. *Nigeria and Its Tin Fields.* London, 1912.
Chief Justice Gollan. "Land Tenure in Northern Nigeria," in *Journal of the Society of Comparative Legislation,* 1902, No. 2, pp. 164 ff.
A. F. Mockler-Ferryman. *British Nigeria.* London, 1902.
E. D. Morel. *Nigeria.* London, 1911.
C. W. J. Orr. *The Making of Northern Nigeria.* London, 1911.
C. H. Robinson. *Nigeria.* London, 1900.
Unsigned. "A Railroad Through Nigeria," in *Bulletin of the American Geographical Society,* November 1907, pp. 668 ff.

NYASALAND

H. L. Duff. *Nyasaland Under the Foreign Office.* London, 1906.

OCEANIA

Georges Bourge. *Les Nouvelles-Hébrides de 1606 à 1906.* Paris, 1906.
Auguste Brunet. *Le Régime International des Nouvelles-Hébrides.* Paris, 1908.
J. W. Burton. *Fiji of Today.* London, 1910.
J. W. Ellison. "The Partition of Samoa: A Study in Imperialism and Diplomacy," in *The Pacific Historical Review,* September 1939, pp. 259 ff.
E. W. Gifford. *Tongan Society.* Honolulu, 1929.
Edward Jacomb. *France and England in the New Hebrides.* Melbourne, 1914.
S. G. C. Knibbs. *The Savage Solomons.* Philadelphia, 1929.
N. S. Politis. *Le Condominium Franco-Anglais des Nouvelles-Hébrides.* Paris, 1908.
R. M. Watson. *A History of Samoa.* Wellington, 1918.

RHODESIA

H. M. Hole. *Old Rhodesian Days.* London, 1928.
P. F. Hone. *Southern Rhodesia.* London, 1909.
H. C. Thomson. *Rhodesia and Its Government.* London, 1898.

SIERRA LEONE

T. G. Alldridge. *A Transformed Colony: Sierra Leone.* London, 1910.
J. J. Crooks. *A History of the Colony of Sierra Leone.* Dublin, 1903.

THE SOUTH AFRICAN PROTECTORATES

W. J. Coope. *Swaziland as an Imperial Factor.* London, 1895.
E. A. T. Dutton. *The Basuto of Basutoland.* London, 1922.
M. Martin. *Basutoland.* London, 1903.
M. F. Perham and L. Curtis. *The Protectorates of South Africa.* London, 1935.

UGANDA

H. H. Johnston. *The Uganda Protectorate.* 2 vols., London, 1904.
F. J. D. Lugard. *The Story of the Uganda Protectorate.* London, 1900.
——————. *Uganda and Its People.* New York, 1901.
G. Roscoe. *The Baganda.* Cambridge, 1911.
A. R. Tucker. *Eighteen Years in Uganda and East Africa.* London, 1911.
Unsigned. "The Uganda Railroad," in *Bulletin of the American Geographical Society,* October and December 1902, pp. 311 ff. and 384 ff.

THE UNION OF SOUTH AFRICA

L. C. M. S. Amery, ed. *The "Times" History of the War in South Africa, 1899-1902.* 7 vols., London, 1900-1909.
R. H. Brand. *The Union of South Africa.* Oxford, 1909.
I. D. Colvin. *South Africa.* London, 1909.
A. C. Doyle. *The Great Boer War.* London, 1903.
Cecil Headlam. "The Milner Period in South Africa," in *The National Review,* May 1932, pp. 585 ff.
Native Races Committee. *The Natives of South Africa.* London, 1901.
J. W. Root. *The South African Labor Question.* Liverpool, 1903.

J. van der Poel. *Railway and Customs Policies in South Africa, 1885-1910.* London, 1933.
W. B. Worsfold. *Lord Milner's Work in South Africa, 1897-1902.* London, 1912.
——————. *The Reconstruction of the New Colonies Under Lord Milner.* 2 vols., London, 1913.

ZANZIBAR
R. N. Lyne. *Zanzibar in Contemporary Times.* London, 1908.

THE DANISH COLONIAL EMPIRE
THE DANISH WEST INDIES
O. P. Austin. *The Danish West Indies, 1621-1901.* Washington, 1902.
A. P. C. Griffin. *A List of Books, With References to Periodicals, on the Danish West Indies.* Washington, 1901.
D. C. Hesseling. *Het Negerhollands der Deense Antillen.* Leiden, 1905.
C. W. Tooke. "The Danish Colonial Fiscal System in the West Indies," in American Economic Association, *Essays in Colonial Finance,* New York, 1900, pp. 144 ff.
Unsigned. "The Danish West Indies," in *The Journal of Geography,* January 1903, pp. 34 ff.
——————. "Notes on the Danish West Indies, an American Gibraltar," in *The National Geographic Magazine,* July 1916, pp. 89 ff.

ICELAND
Nelson Annandale. *The Faroes and Iceland: Studies in Island Life.* Oxford, 1905.
Sven Jansen. *Iceland Today.* London, 1906.
Lewis Johnson. *Iceland's Fisheries.* London, 1912.
V. K. Kalan. *Iceland and the Icelanders.* Grenoble, 1914.

THE FRENCH COLONIAL EMPIRE
GENERAL
J. F. Archibald. "In Civilized French Africa," in *The National Geographic Magazine,* March 1909, pp. 303 ff.
Pierre Aubry. *La Colonisation et les Colonies.* Paris, 1909.
F. Bernard. *Pourquoi et Comment Coloniser?* Paris, 1905.
M. Betham-Edwards. *In French Africa.* London, 1912.
A. Billiard. *Politique et Organisation Coloniales: Principes Généraux.* Paris, 1899.
A. Bonnefoy-Sibour. *Le Pouvoir Législatif aux Colonies.* Dijon, 1908.
E. Bouchié de Belle. *Le Régime Financier des Colonies.* Paris, 1903.
J. P. Boulard. *Etude Juridique et Critique des Conseils Généraux des Colonies Françaises.* Toulouse, 1902.
J. C. Bracq. "The Colonial Expansion of France," in *The National Geographic Magazine,* June 1900, pp. 225 ff.
G. Capus and D. Bois. *Les Produits Coloniaux.* Paris, 1912.
L. Cario and C. Régismanset. *La Concurrence des Colonies à la Métropole.* Paris, 1906.
Joseph Chailley-Bert. *Dix Années de Politique Coloniale.* Paris, 1902.
Albert Cousin. *Concession Coloniale: Droits et Obligations en Résultant.* Paris, 1899.
P. Denizet. *Les Banques Coloniales.* Paris, 1899.
E. A. de Renty. *Les Chemins de Fer Coloniaux en Afrique.* 3 vols., Paris, 1903-1905.
M. Dubois and A. Terrier. *Les Colonies Françaises.* Paris, 1902.
V. Dupuich. *Le Régime Législatif des Colonies Françaises.* Paris, 1912.
Robert Ermels. *Frankreichs koloniale Handelspolitik.* Berlin, 1910.
Eugène Fallex and Alphonse Mairey. *La France et ses Colonies au Début du XXe Siècle.* Paris, 1914.
E. Ferry. *La France en Afrique.* Paris, 1905.
Georges François. *Le Budget Local des Colonies.* Paris, 1903.
Edmond Gaudart. *Le Régime Financier des Colonies Françaises.* Paris, 1911.
F. Geoffroy. *L'Organisation Judiciaire des Colonies Françaises.* Paris, 1915.
Arthur Girault. *The Colonial Tariff Policy of France.* Oxford, 1916.
André Goumain-Cornille. *Les Banques Coloniales.* Paris, 1903.
P. Grenier. *L'Armée Coloniale.* Paris, 1902.
Camille Guy. *Les Colonies Françaises.* Paris, 1900.
Gabriel Hanotaux. *Fachoda.* Paris, 1909.

Alfred Hignette. *Le Crédit dans les Colonies Sucrières Françaises.* Paris, 1901.
Charles Humbert. *L'Oeuvre Française aux Colonies.* Paris, 1913.
Albert Laporte. *Le Problème Monétaire dans les Vieilles Colonies.* Paris, 1908.
André Lebon. *La Politique de la France en Afrique, 1896-1898: Mission Marchand, Niger, Madagascar.* Paris, 1901.
J. le Bourdais des Touches. *Le Régime Financier des Colonies Françaises.* Paris, 1898.
Henri Lorin. *La France, Puissance Coloniale.* Paris, 1906.
André Maurois. "L'Angleterre et Fachoda," in *Revue de Paris,* February 15, 1934, pp. 721 ff.
O. F. Meynier. *L'Afrique Noire.* Paris, 1911.
Paul Pelet. *Atlas des Colonies Françaises.* Paris, 1914.
C. Perreau. *Le Régime Commercial des Colonies Françaises.* Paris, 1903.
M. Perrot et al. *Les Grands Produits Végétaux des Colonies Françaises.* Paris, 1915.
C. W. Porter. *The Career of Théophile Delcassé.* Philadelphia, 1936.
Charles Régismanset. *Questions Coloniales, 1900-1912.* Paris, 1912.
Charles Rotté. *Les Chemins de Fer et Tramways des Colonies.* Paris, 1910.
E. R. Seligman. "The French Colonial System," in American Economic Association, *Essays in Colonial Finance,* New York, 1900, pp. 20 ff.
Octave Thomas. *Nos Colonies et le Budget Métropolitain.* Paris, 1906.

ALGERIA

M. Ajam. *Problèmes Algériens.* Paris, 1913.
R. J. Aynard. *L'Oeuvre Française en Algérie.* Paris, 1913.
Edgar Berman. *French North Africa.* London, 1911.
A. Bernard. *Les Confins Algéro-Marocains.* Paris, 1911.
Victor Demontès. *Le Peuple Algérien.* Algiers, 1906.
Roy Devereux. *Aspects of Algeria: Historical—Political—Colonial.* New York, 1912.
E. Doutté and A. Bernard. *Enquête sur la Dispersion de la Langue Berbère en Algérie.* Paris, 1913.
E. F. Gautier. *Sahara Algérien.* Paris, 1912.
Gilbert Jacqueton. *Algérie et Tunisie.* Paris, 1906.
M. Jais. *La Banque de l'Algérie et le Crédit Agricole.* Paris, 1902.
Henri Lorin. *L'Afrique du Nord: Tunisie-Algérie-Maroc.* Paris, 1913.
Gaston Loth. *Le Peuplement Italien en Tunisie et en Algérie.* Paris, 1905.
André Mallarmé. *L'Organisation Gouvernementale de l'Algérie.* Paris, 1901.
P. de Massougnes. *Le Régime Commercial de l'Algérie.* Paris, 1901.
Ernest Mercier. *La Question Indigène en Algérie au Commencement du XXe Siècle.* Paris, 1901.
P. Mohr. *Algerien.* Berlin, 1907.
Marcel Morand. *Etudes de Droit Musulman Algérien.* Algiers, 1910.
Onésime Reclus. *Algérie et Tunisie.* Paris, 1909.
M. Schanz. *Algerien, Tunesien, Tripolitanien.* Halle, 1905.
Doctor Sèbe. *La Conscription des Indigènes d'Algérie.* Paris, 1912.
Unsigned. "Progress in the Algerian Sahara," in *Bulletin of the American Geographical Society,* January 1908, pp. 19 ff.
Henri Vast. *L'Algérie et les Colonies Françaises.* Paris, 1901.
Maurice Wahl. *L'Algérie.* Paris, 1908.

FRENCH AMERICA

Emile Alcindor. *Les Antilles Françaises: Leur Assimilation Politique à la Métropole.* Paris, 1899.
P. Bernissant. *Etude sur le Régime Agricole des Antilles Françaises.* Paris, 1916.
Felix Billot. *L'Ouverture du Canal de Panama et les Intérêts des Colonies Françaises des Antilles et d'Océanie.* Paris, 1913.
Maurice Caperon. *Saint-Pierre et Miquelon.* Paris, 1900.
P. Chemin-Dupontès. *Les Petites Antilles.* Paris, 1909.
Albert Duchêne. *Les Banques Coloniales des Antilles, de la Réunion et de la Guyane.* Paris, 1909.
Jean Duchesne-Fournet. *La Main-d'Oeuvre dans les Guyanes.* Paris, 1905.
Paul Guiral. *L'Immigration Réglementée aux Antilles Françaises et à la Réunion.* Paris, 1911.
Alfred Hignette. *Le Crédit dans les Colonies Sucrières Françaises.* Paris, 1901.
Hermann Koefer. *L'Archipel de la Guadeloupe et son Importance Economique.* Paris, 1910.

Emile Légier. *La Martinique et la Guadeloupe.* Paris, 1905.
Maurice Legon. *Nos Antilles.* Paris, 1901.
Paul Reinsch. "French Experience with Representative Government in the West Indies," in *The American Historical Review,* April 1901, pp. 475 ff.
Justin Rovel. *Le Régime Politique et Législatif des Antilles Françaises.* Nancy, 1902.
André Souply. *Etude sur l'Octroi de Mer à la Guadeloupe, à la Martinique et à la Réunion.* Paris, 1912.
Paul Werner. *Martinique* .... Bonn, 1910.

FRENCH EQUATORIAL AFRICA

Georges Bruel. *Bibliographie de l'Afrique Equatoriale Française.* Paris, 1914.
———. *Géographie de l'Afrique Equatoriale Française.* Paris, 1916.
F. Challaye. *Le Congo Français.* Paris, 1909.
France. Gouvernement Général de l'Afrique Equatoriale Française. *L'Evolution Economique des Possessions Françaises de l'Afrique Equatoriale.* Paris, 1913.
Mission d'Etudes de la Maladie du Sommeil au Congo Français. *Rapport.* Paris, 1909.
V. Pourbaix. *Le Régime Economique et les Sociétés Commerciales du Congo Français.* Brussels, 1899.
Captain Renard. *La Colonisation au Congo Français.* Paris, 1901.
Fernand Rouget. *L'Expansion Coloniale au Congo Français.* Paris, 1906.
André Servel. *Organisation Administrative et Financière de l'Afrique Equatoriale Française.* Paris, 1912.
Unsigned. *L'Evolution Economique des Possessions Françaises de l'Afrique Equatoriale.* Paris, 1913.

THE FRENCH ESTABLISHMENTS IN INDIA

G. B. Malleson. *A History of the French in India.* Edinburgh, 1909.
Alfred Martineau and M. A. Leblond. *Côte Française des Somalis. Inde Française. La Réunion.* Paris, 1931.

FRENCH SOMALILAND

Henri le Pointe. *La Colonisation Française au Pays des Somalis.* Paris, 1917.
Alfred Martineau and M. A. Leblond. *Côte Française des Somalis. Inde Française. La Réunion.* Paris, 1931.
J. B. Piolet and C. Noufflard. *L'Empire Colonial de la France: Madagascar, la Réunion, Mayotte, les Comores, Djibouti.* Paris, 1900.

FRENCH WEST AFRICA

André Arcin. *Histoire de la Guinée Française.* Paris, 1911.
———. *La Guinée Française.* Paris, 1907.
A. E. A. Baratier. *A Travers l'Afrique.* Paris, 1912. [French colonial enterprise in Senegal, Sudan and Ivory Coast.]
———. *Epopées Africaines.* Paris, 1912. [The French in West Africa.]
Augustin Bernard and N. Lacroix. *La Pénétration Saharienne, 1830-1906.* Algiers, 1906.
M. Beurdeley. *La Justice Indigène en Afrique Occidentale Française.* Paris, 1916.
Maurice Cortier. *D'une Rive à l'Autre du Sahara.* Paris, 1908.
A. d'Anfreville de la Salle. *Notre Vieux Sénégal.* Paris, 1909.
Maurice Delafosse. *Haut Sénégal-Niger (Soudan Français).* 3 vols., Paris, 1912.
A. de Salinis. *Le Protectorat Français sur la Côte des Esclaves* [Dahomey]. Paris, 1908.
Felix Dubois. *Notre Beau Niger.* Paris, 1911.
———. *Timbuctoo the Mysterious.* London, 1899.
Jules Emily. *Fachoda: Mission Marchand, 1896-1899.* Paris, 1935.
———. *Mission Marchand: Journal de Route* .... Paris, 1913.
G. François. *Le Gouvernement Général de l'Afrique Occidentale Française.* Paris, 1908.
———. *Notre Colonie du Dahomey: Sa Formation—son Développement—son Avenir.* Paris, 1906.
Colonel Gouraud. *Le Pacification de la Mauritanie.* Paris, 1911.
A. Gruvel. *L'Industrie des Pêches sur la Côte Occidentale d'Afrique.* Paris, 1913.
T. Henry. *Le Coton dans l'Afrique Occidentale Française.* Paris, 1904.
M. Lemée. *Enseignement en Afrique Occidentale.* Paris, 1906.
P. Lemoine. *Afrique Occidentale.* Heidelberg, 1913.
P. Leroy-Beaulieu. *Le Sahara, le Soudan et les Chemins de Fer Transsahariens.* Paris, 1904.

C. P. Lucas and A. B. Keith. *West Africa.* Oxford, 1913.
M. Marty. *Les Tribus de la Haute Mauritanie.* Paris, 1915.
Marcel Olivier. *Le Sénégal.* Paris, 1907.
Charles Rabot. "The French Conquest of the Sahara," in *The National Geographic Magazine,* February 1905, pp. 76 ff.
Fernand Rouget. *La Guinée Française.* Corbeil, 1906.
R. P. A. Sebire. *Les Plantes Utiles du Sénégal.* Paris, 1899.
Louis Sonolet. *L'Afrique Occidentale Française.* Paris, 1913.
Louis Tauxier. *Le Noir du Soudan.* Paris, 1912.
Auguste Terrier. *L'Oeuvre de la Troisième République en Afrique Occidentale.* Paris, 1910.
Captain Touchard. *Travaux et Reconnaissances de Pénétration Saharienne.* Paris, 1907.
Unsigned. *Chemins de Fer de l'Afrique Occidentale.* 3 vols., Paris, 1906.
———. *Service Médical au Haut Sénégal-Niger.* Paris, 1906.
Georges Widal. *La France en Afrique Occidentale Française.* Paris, 1910.
———, ed. *Conférence sur la France en Afrique Occidentale des Origines à nos Jours.* Paris, 1910.

THE INDO-CHINESE UNION

G. E. Anderson. "Cochin China," in *Journal of the American Asiatic Association,* July 1911, p. 177.
Etienne Aymonier. *Le Cambodge.* 3 vols., Paris, 1900-1904.
Paul Beau. *Situation de l'Indochine de 1902-07.* 2 vols., Saïgon, 1908.
F. Bernard. *L'Indochine.* Paris, 1901.
A. Boudillon. *Le Régime de la Propriété Foncière en Indochine.* Paris, 1915.
Henri Brenier. *Essai d'Atlas Statistique de l'Indochine Française.* Hanoï, 1914.
J. E. Conner. "The Forgotten Ruins of Indo-China," in *The National Geographic Magazine,* March 1912, pp. 209 ff.
Henri Cordier. *Biblioteca Indosinica.* 4 vols., Paris, 1912-1915.
———. *La France et l'Angleterre en Indochine et en Chine sous le Premier Empire.* Paris, 1903.
J. C. G. Courtellemont. *L'Indochine.* Paris, 1902.
P. Cultru. *Histoire de la Cochinchine Française.* Paris, 1910.
A. Cunningham. *The French in Tonkin and South China.* London, 1902.
Lucien de Reinach. *Le Laos.* 2 vols., Paris, 1911.
E. Diguet. *Annam et Indochine Française.* Paris, 1908.
———. *Les Annamites.* Paris, 1906.
J. Dupuis. *Le Tonkin de 1872 à 1886.* Paris, 1910.
L. Faque. *L'Indochine Française.* Paris, 1910.
Albert Gaisman. *L'Oeuvre de la France au Tonkin.* Paris, 1906.
Doctor Gay-Lugny. *Le Commerce Extérieur de l'Indochine.* Paris, 1910.
C. Gosselin. *L'Empire Annam.* Paris, 1904.
———. *Le Laos et le Protectorat Français.* Paris, 1900.
Alleyne Ireland. *The Far Eastern Tropics* [Including French Indo-China]. Boston, 1905.
Adhémard Leclère. *Histoire du Cambodge.* Paris, 1914.
Camille LeJeune. *Régime de la Propriété Foncière en Pays Annamite.* Paris, 1904.
Charles Lemire. *Les Cinque Pays de l'Indochine Française.* Paris, 1900.
A. Neton. *L'Indochine et son Avenir Economique.* Paris. 1904.
P. Nicolas. *La Vie Française en Cochinchine.* Paris, 1900.
M. Peyrouton. *Les Monopoles en Indochine.* Paris, 1912.
E. Picanon. *Le Laos Français.* Paris, 1900.
H. E. Russier. *Histoire Sommaire du Royaume de Cambodge.* Saïgon, 1916.
——— and Henri Brenier. *L'Indochine Française.* Saïgon, 1915.
L. Salaun. *Essai sur l'Organisation de l'Indochine.* Hanoï, 1901.
Alfred Schreiner. *Abrégé de l'Histoire d'Annam.* Saïgon, 1906.
Unsigned. *L'Assistance Médicale en Indochine.* Paris, 1911.
———. *Mémoire Relatif au Régime Monétaire de l'Indochine.* Paris, 1914.

MADAGASCAR

Louis Brunet. *L'Oeuvre de la France à Madagascar.* Paris, 1903.
A. d'Anfreville de la Salle. *Madagascar.* Paris, 1902.

J. S. Galliéni. *Lettres de Madagascar, 1896-1905.* Paris, 1928.
———————. *Mémoires du Général Galliéni.* Paris, 1920.
———————. *Neuf Ans à Madagascar.* Paris, 1908.
E. F. Gautier. *Madagascar.* Paris, 1902.
Guillaume Grandidier. *Bibliographie de Madagascar.* 1 vol. in 2 parts, Paris, 1905-1906.
———————. *Bibliographie de Madagascar, 1904-1933.* Paris, 1936.
———————. *Madagascar au Début du XXe Siècle.* Paris, 1902.
W. H. Hunt. "Madagascar," in *Bulletin of the American Geographical Society,* 1900, pp. 297 ff.
G. Julien. *Institutions Politiques et Sociales de Madagascar.* 2 vols., Paris, 1909.
Konrad Keller. *Madagascar, Mauritius and the Other East-African Islands.* London, 1901.
F. X. Loisy. *Madagascar: Etude Economique.* Paris, 1914.
E. O. MacMahon. *Christian Missions in Madagascar.* Westminster, 1914.
Gustave Mondain. *Une Courte Histoire de Christianisme à Madagascar.* Paris, 1916.
J. B. Piolet and C. Noufflard. *L'Empire Colonial de la France: Madagascar, la Réunion, Mayotte, les Comores, Djibouti.* Paris, 1900.
André You. *Madagascar: Histoire, Organisation, Colonisation.* Paris, 1905.
Graf zu Pappenheim. *Madagaskar.* Berlin, 1906.

MOROCCO, INCLUDING THE INTERNATIONAL CITY OF TANGIER

Emile Amar. *L'Organisation de la Propriété Foncière au Maroc.* Paris, 1913.
E. N. Anderson. *The First Moroccan Crisis, 1904-1906.* Chicago, 1930.
Ellis Ashmead-Bartlett. *The Passing of the Shereefian Empire.* Edinburgh, 1910.
Victor Bérard. *L'Affaire Marocaine.* Paris, 1906.
Stephane Berge. *La Justice Française au Maroc.* Paris, 1917.
Augustin Bernard. *Les Confins Algéro-Marocains.* Paris, 1911.
T. L. Blayney. "A Journey in Morocco, the Land of the Moors," in *The National Geographic Magazine,* August 1911, pp. 750 ff.
J. Colomb. *Le Régime Financier du Maroc.* Paris, 1914.
Albert Cousin. *Le Maroc.* Paris, 1905.
Leon Deloncle. *Le Statut International du Maroc.* Paris, 1912.
Gustav Diercks. *Die Marokkofrage und die Konferenz von Algeciras.* Berlin, 1906.
Emile Dubuisson. *Le Maroc: Géographie, Types et Coutumes.* Melun, 1908.
France. Ministry of Foreign Affairs. *Affaires du Maroc, 1901-1912.* 6 vols., Paris, 1905-1912.
Louis Gentil. *Le Maroc Physique.* Paris, 1912.
Maurice Gentil. *La Procédure Civile au Maroc.* Bordeaux, 1916.
André Gourdin. *La Politique Française au Maroc.* Paris, 1906.
Fritz Hartung. "Die englische Politik in der Morokkokrise des Jahres 1911," in *Berliner Monatsheft,* August 1932, pp. 752 ff.
Georges Jary. *Les Intérêts de la France au Maroc.* Paris, 1911.
André Leblanc. *La Politique Européenne au Maroc à l'Epoque Contemporaine.* Paris, 1906.
Henri Lorin. *L'Afrique du Nord: Tunisie-Algérie-Maroc.* Paris, 1913.
Doctor Mauran. *Le Maroc d'Aujourd'hui et de Demain.* Paris, 1909.
———————. *La Société Marocaine.* Paris, 1909.
L. Maurice. *La Politique Marocaine de l'Allemagne.* Paris, 1916.
André Maurois. *Lyautey.* New York, 1931.
Budgett Meakin. *The Moorish Empire.* London, 1899.
Paul Mohr. *Marokko.* Berlin, 1902.
Frederick Moore. *The Passing of Morocco.* Boston, 1908.
E. D. Morel. *Morocco in Diplomacy.* London, 1912.
Ion Perdicaris. "Morocco, the Land of the Extreme West," in *The National Geographic Magazine,* March 1906, pp. 117 ff.
Raymond Recouly. "Agadir," in *Revue de France,* February 15, 1932, pp. 611 ff.
———————. "Tangier: Le Crise de 1905," in *Revue de France,* February 1, 1932, pp. 415 ff.
Etienne Richet. *La Politique Allemande au Maroc.* Paris, 1917.
E. Rouard de Card. *La Question Marocaine et la Négociation Franco-Espagnole de 1902.* Paris, 1912.
———————. ed. *Documents Diplomatiques pour Servir à l'Etude de la Question Marocaine.* Paris, 1911.
———————. *Traites et Accords Concernant le Protectorat de la France au Maroc.* Paris, 1914.

Bertel Taerdon. *The Origins of French Morocco, 1898-1912.* Zurich, 1915.
Luther Taibor. *The Peoples and Resources of French Morocco.* London, 1913.
André Tardieu. *La Conférence d'Algésiras.* Paris, 1909.
Unsigned. *L'Essor Industriel à Casablanca.* Paris, 1914.
——————. *Le Mystère d'Agadir.* Paris, 1912.
Fernand Vatin. *Le Maroc Physique, Economique, Politique.* Paris, 1907.

OCEANIA[1]

J. B. Alberti. *Etude sur la Colonisation à la Nouvelle-Caledonie.* Paris, 1909.
Felix Billot. *L'Ouverture du Canal de Panama et les Intérêts des Colonies Françaises des Antilles et d'Océanie.* Paris, 1913.
J. Blanc. *Les Iles Wallis.* Paris, 1914.
René Bonhoure. *La Propriété Foncière dans les Etablissements Français de l'Océanie.* Paris, 1915.
Georges Bourge. *Les Nouvelles-Hébrides de 1606 à 1906.* Paris, 1906.
Auguste Brunet. *Le Régime International des Nouvelles-Hébrides.* Paris, 1908.
F. W. Christian. *Eastern Pacific Lands: Tahiti and the Marquesas Islands.* London, 1910.
M. Deniau. *Conférence sur les Missions d'Océanie.* Chartres, 1900.
France. Bibliothèque Nationale. *Catalogue de l'Histoire de l'Océanie.* Paris, 1912.
Edward Jacomb. *France and England in the New Hebrides.* Melbourne, 1914.
N. S. Politis. *Le Condominium Franco-Anglais des Nouvelles-Hébrides.* Paris, 1908.

REUNION

Hubert J. de Cordemoy. *Etudes sur l'Ile de la Réunion.* Paris, 1904.
Albert Duchêne. *Les Banques Coloniales des Antilles, de la Réunion et de la Guyane.* Paris, 1909.
Paul Guiral. *L'Immigration Réglementée aux Antilles Françaises et à la Réunion.* Paris, 1911.
Alfred Martineau and M. A. Leblond. *Côte Française des Somalis. Inde Française. La Réunion.* Paris, 1931.
J. B. Piolet and C. Noufflard. *L'Empire Colonial de la France: Madagascar, la Réunion, Mayotte, les Comores, Djibouti.* Paris, 1900.
André Souply. *Etude sur l'Octroi de Mer à la Guadeloupe, à la Martinique et à la Réunion.* Paris, 1912.

TUNIS

Jacques Bahar. *Le Protectorat Tunisien.* Paris, 1904.
A. d'Anthouard. *Réflexions sur notre Politique Coloniale en Tunisie.* Paris, 1914.
P. H. Decker-David. *L'Agriculture Indigène en Tunisie.* Tunis, 1912.
Camille Fidel. *Les Intérêts Italiens en Tunisie.* Paris, 1911.
B. Hofstetter. *Die Vorgeschichte des franzoesischen Protektorats in Tunis bis zum Bardovertrag.* Bern, 1914.
Gilbert Jacqueton. *Algérie et Tunisie.* Paris, 1906.
F. E. Johnson. "Tunis of Today," in *The National Geographic Magazine,* August 1911, pp. 723 ff.
Henri Lorin. *L'Afrique du Nord: Tunisie-Algérie-Maroc.* Paris, 1913.
Gaston Loth. *La Tunisie et l'Oeuvre du Protectorat Français.* Paris, 1907.
——————. *Le Peuplement Italien en Tunisie et en Algérie.* Paris, 1905.
J. Lulvès. "Auf welche Weise machte sich Frankreich zum Herrn von Tunis?", in *Deutsche Revue,* February 1915, pp. 125 ff.
Hans Plehn. "Die Methoden der franzoesischen Politik bei der Erwerbung Tunesiens," in *Zeitschrift fuer Politik,* 1914, pp. 1 ff.
Onésime Reclus. *Algérie et Tunisie.* Paris, 1909.
Jules Saurin. *L'Invasion Sicilienne et le Peuplement Français de la Tunisie.* Paris, 1900.
M. Schanz. *Algerien, Tunesien, Tripolitanien.* Halle, 1905.
Andrea Torre. "Come la Francia s'Impadroni di Tunisi," in *Rivista di Roma,* April-May 1899, pp. 64 ff.
Fernand Vatin. *Les Chemins de Fer en Tunisie.* Paris, 1905.

---

[1] This includes the following political units: French Establishments in Oceania, New Caledonia, the New Hebrides Condominium and the Wallis and Futuna Islands.

THE GERMAN COLONIAL EMPIRE

GENERAL

F. Baltzer. *Die Kolonialbahnen.* Berlin, 1916.
Moritz Bonn. "German Colonial Policy," in *United Empire,* February 1914, pp. 126 ff.
Maximilian Brose. *Die deutsche Koloniallitteratur im Jahre 1896-1913.* 18 vols., Berlin, 1897-1914.
André Chéradame. *La Colonisation et les Colonies Allemandes.* Paris, 1905.
Adolph Coppius. *Hamburgs Bedeutung auf dem Gebiet der deutschen Kolonialpolitik.* Berlin, 1905.
P. Decharme. *Compagnies et Sociétés Coloniales Allemandes.* Paris, 1903.
B. Dernburg. *Zielpunkte des deutschen Kolonialwesens.* Berlin, 1907.
Max Eckert. *Wirtschafts Atlas der deutschen Kolonieen.* Berlin, 1912.
R. Fitzner. *Deutsches Kolonialhandbuch.* 2 vols., Berlin, 1901 (Supplements in 1902, 1904 and 1905).
F. Florack. *Die Schutzgebiete: ihre Organisation in Verfassung und Verwaltung.* Tuebingen, 1905.
Kurt Hassert. *Deutschlands Kolonien.* Leipzig, 1910.
Adolf Heilborn. *Die deutschen Kolonien.* Leipzig, 1906.
A. G. Keller. "The Colonial Policy of the Germans," in *The Yale Review,* February 1902, pp. 390 ff.
Otto Koebner. *Einfuehrung in die Kolonialpolitik.* Jena, 1908.
I. Loeb. "The German Colonial Fiscal System," in American Economic Association, *Essays in Colonial Finance.* New York, 1900, pp. 40 ff.
G. Meinecke. *Die deutschen Kolonien in Wort und Bild.* Leipzig, 1900.
Hans Meyer, ed. *Das deutsche Kolonialreich.* 2 vols., Leipzig, 1909-1910.
C. Mirbt. *Missionen in Kolonialpolitik in den deutschen Schutzgebieten.* Tuebingen, 1910.
E. L. Radlauer. *Die lokale Selbstverwaltung der kolonialen Finanzen.* Breslau, 1909.
H. Riebow *et al.,* eds. *Die deutsche Kolonialgesetzgebung.* 10 vols., Berlin, 1893-1910.
Paul Rohrbach. *Das deutsche Kolonialwesen.* Leipzig, 1911.
——————. *Deutsche Kolonialwirtschaft.* Berlin, 1909.
——————. *Die deutsche Kolonien.* Dachau, 1914.
——————. *Unsere koloniale Zukunftsarbeit.* Stuttgart, 1915.
K. Schwabe. *Die deutschen Kolonien.* 2 vols., Berlin, 1914.
——————. *Kriegfuehrung in den Kolonien.* Berlin, 1903.
H. See. *Die deutsche Kolonialgesellschaft, 1882-1907.* Berlin, 1908.
August Seidel. *Deutschlands Kolonien.* Berlin, 1902.
M. Slunk. *Das Schulwesen in den deutschen Schutzgebieten.* Hamburg, 1914.
J. K. Vietor. *Geschichtliche und kulturelle Entwickelung unser Schutzgebiete.* Berlin, 1913.
A. von der Heydt. *Kolonialhandbuch.* Berlin, 1913.
Alfred Zimmermann. *Die Geschichte der deutschen Kolonialpolitik.* Berlin, 1914.
——————. *Kolonialpolitik.* Leipzig, 1905.
P. K. Zorn. *Deutsche Kolonialgesetzgebung.* Berlin, 1913.

THE BAGDAD RAILWAY PROJECT

Ewald Banse. *Auf den Spuren der Bagdadbahn.* Weimar, 1913.
André Chéradame. *Le Chemin de Fer de Bagdad.* Paris, 1915.
E. M. Earle. *Turkey, the Great Powers and the Bagdad Railway.* New York, 1923.
S. B. Fay. "The Bagdad Railway: A German Defense of the Financial Arrangements," in *The Journal of Modern History,* June 1932, pp. 240 ff.
F. R. Maunsell. "The Damascus to Mecca Line: One Thousand Miles of Railway Built for Pilgrims and not for Dividends," in *The National Geographic Magazine,* February 1909, pp. 156 ff.
Georges Mazel. *Le Chemin de Fer de Bagdad.* Montpellier, 1911.
Louis Ragey. *La Question du Chemin de Fer de Bagdad, 1893-1914.* Paris, 1936.
Paul Rohrbach. *Die Bagdadbahn.* Berlin, 1911.
Arthur von Gwinner. "The Bagdad Railway and the Question of British Cooperation," in *The Nineteenth Century,* June 1909, pp. 1083 ff.

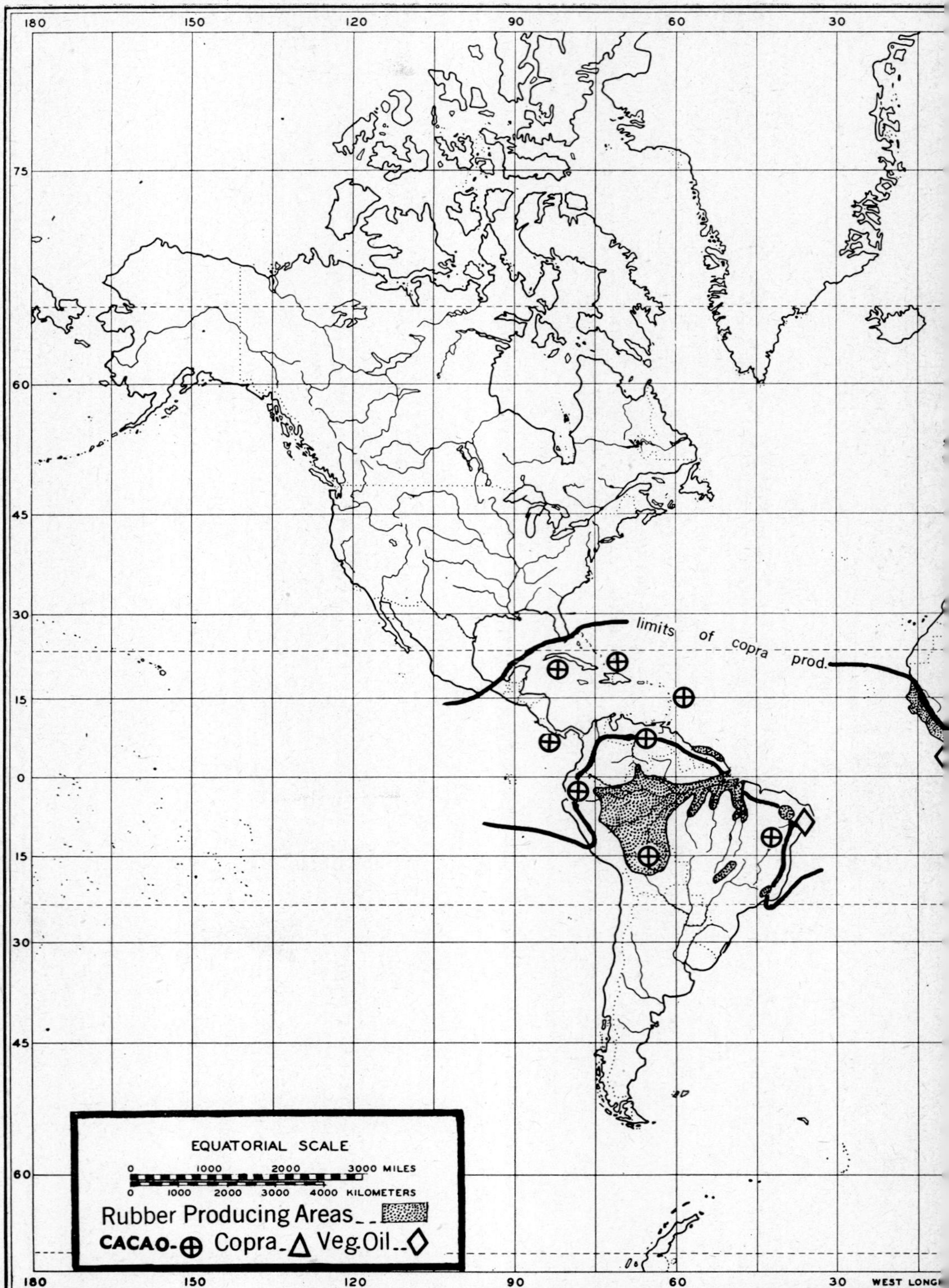

Tropical Commod

limits of copra prod.

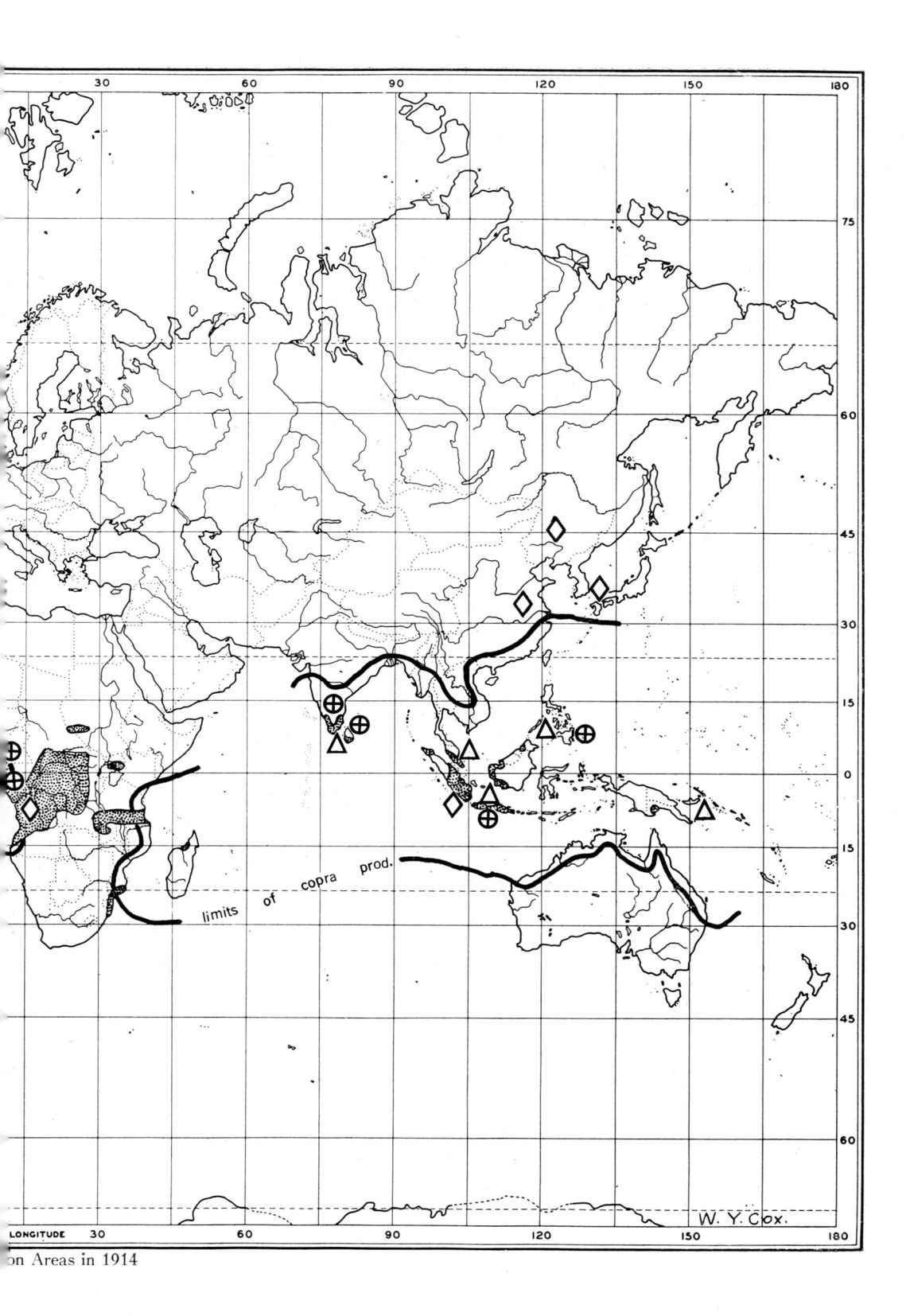

W. Y. Cox.

on Areas in 1914

THE EAST INDIES, KIAOCHOW AND THE PACIFIC BASIN

H. Blum. *Neu-Guinea und der Bismarck-Archipel.* Berlin, 1900.
F. W. Christian. *The Caroline Islands.* London, 1899.
A. Kraemer. *Die samoa Inseln.* 3 vols., Stuttgart, 1902-1903.
M. Krieger. *Neu-Guinea.* Berlin, 1899.
Richard Neuhauss. *Deutsch Neu-Guinea.* 3 vols., Berlin, 1911.
F. Richthofen. *Schantung und seine Eingangspforte Kiautschou.* Berlin, 1898.
Heinrich Schnee. *Bilder aus der Suedsee: unter den kannibalischen Staemmen des Bismarck-Archipels.* Berlin, 1904.
L. W. Schrameier. *Aus Kiautschous Verwaltung.* Jena, 1914.
————. *Kiautschou.* Berlin, 1915.
Wilhelm Sievers. *Die Schutzgebiete in der Suedsee.* 2 vols., Leipzig, 1910.
Unsigned. "The Caroline Islands," in *The Journal of School Geography,* September 1899, pp. 262 ff.
Ernst von Hesse-Wartegg. *Samoa, Bismarck-Archipel und Neu-Guinea.* Leipzig, 1902.
————. *Schantung und Deutsch-China.* Leipzig, 1898.
S. J. von Prowazek. *Die Deutschen Marianen.* Leipzig, 1913.

GERMAN EAST AFRICA

Gustavo Chiesi. *La Colonizzazione Europea nell Est Africa: Italia-Inghilterra-Germania.* Turin, 1909.
H. Fonck. *Deutsch-Ostafrika.* Berlin, 1909.
Eugène Plumon. *La Colonie Allemande de l'Afrique Orientale et la Politique de l'Allemagne dans ces Régions.* Rennes, 1905.
P. Samassa. *Die Besiedlung Deutsch-Ostafrikas.* Berlin, 1909.
Graf von Pfeil. *Zur Erwerbung von Deutsch-Ostafrika.* Berlin, 1907.

GERMAN SOUTHWEST AFRICA

A. F. Calvert. *Southwest Africa During the German Occupation, 1884-1914.* London, 1916.
Paul Leutwein. *Afrikanerschicksal: Gouverneur Leutwein [von Suedwest-Afrika] und seine Zeit.* Stuttgart, 1929.
T. Leutwein. *Elf Jahre Gouverneur in Deutsch Suedwest-Afrika.* Berlin, 1908.
Erich Quiring. *Die Eisenbahnen Deutsch Suedwest-Afrikas und ihre Bedeutung fuer die Wirtschaftliche Entwickelung der Kolonie.* Erlangen, 1911.
Theodor Rehbock. *Deutschlands Pflichten in Deutsch Suedwest-Afrika.* Berlin, 1904.
Paul Rohrbach. *Dernburg und die Suedwest-Afrikaner.* Berlin, 1911.
————. *Suedwest-Afrika.* Berlin, 1907.
L. Sander. *Geschichte der Deutschen Suedwest-Afrika Kolonialgesellschaft.* Berlin, 1912.
Kurd Schwabe. *Der Krieg in Deutsch Suedwest-Afrika, 1904-1906.* Berlin, 1907.
————. *Deutsch Suedwest-Afrika.* Berlin, 1905.
————. *Im Deutschen Diamantenlande [: German Southwest Africa].* Berlin, 1909.
————. *Mit Schwert und Pflug in Deutsch Suedwest-Afrika.* Berlin, 1904.

TOGO AND KAMERUN

A. F. Calvert. *The Cameroons.* London, 1917.
————. *Togoland.* London, 1918.
H. Klose. *Togo unter deutscher Flagge: Reisebilder und Betrachtungen.* Berlin, 1899.
Camille Martin. *Togo et Cameroun.* Paris, 1916.

THE ITALIAN COLONIAL EMPIRE

GENERAL

Alberto Botarelli. *Compendio di Storia Coloniale Italiana.* Rome, 1914.
A. Dauzat. *L'Expansion Italienne.* Paris, 1914.
Palo de Vecchis. *Italy's Civilizing Mission in Africa.* New York, 1912.
Direzione Centrale degli Affari Coloniali. *Raccolta di Pubblicazioni Coloniali Italiane.* Rome, 1911.
W. C. Hill. *Select Bibliography of Publications on Foreign Colonisation . . . Italian (etc.) . . . .* London, 1915.

A. G. Keller. "Italy's Experience with Colonies," in American Economic Association, *Essays in Colonial Finance*. New York, 1900, pp. 105 ff.
Roberto Michels. *L'Imperialismo Italiano*. Milan, 1914.
C. Rossetti. *Il Regime Monetario delle Colonie Italiane*. Rome, 1914.
Tommaso Tittoni. *Italy's Foreign and Colonial Policy*. London, 1914.

ERITREA

Ezio Marchi. *Studi sulla Pastorizia della Colonia Eritrea*. Florence, 1910.
A. M. Tancredi. *Notizie e Studi sulla Colonia Eritrea*. Rome, 1913.
Unsigned. "A Cotton Growing Project in Eritrea, Italian Africa," in *The Pan-American Magazine,* September 1911, pp. 310.

LIBYA (TRIPOLITANIA AND CYRENAICA)

J. Assada. *La Tripolitaine*. Paris, 1912.
F. Bac. *L'Aventure Italienne*. Paris, 1912.
T. Barclay. *The Turco-Italian War and Its Problems*. London, 1912.
Domenico Bartolotti. *La Colonizzazione Militaire in Libia*. Padua, 1914.
W. H. Beehler. *The History of the Italian-Turkish War (1911-1912)*. Annapolis, n.d.
Ethel Braun. *The New Tripoli*. London, 1914.
Ugo Ceccherini. *Bibliografia della Libia*. Rome, 1915. (Continuing Federico Minutilli's work, q.v. in this same section).
Socrate Checchi. *Attraverso la Cirenaica*. Rome, 1912.
R. Corselli. *Le Nuove Terre Italiane nella Libia*. Rome, 1912.
L. Cufino. *La Tripolitania*. Naples, 1906.
——————. *Un Contributo alla Bibliografia della Tripolitania*. Naples, 1912.
——————. *Secondo Contributo* . . . . Naples, 1912.
H. M. de Mathuisieulx. *La Tripolitaine d'Hier et de Demain*. Paris, 1912.
Ansonio Franzoni. *Colonizzazione e Proprietà Fondiaria in Libia*. Rome, 1912.
H. Froidevaux. *Tripolitaine*. Paris, 1912.
G. Garibaldi-Farina. *L'Avvenire della Libia*. Rome, 1914.
L. Goretti. *La Cirenaica*. Rome, 1911.
Tullio Irace. *With the Italians in Tripoli*. London, 1912.
W. Kalbskopf. *Die Aussenpolitik der Mittelmaechte im Tripoliskrieg und die letzte Dreibunderneuerung, 1911-1912*. Erlangen, 1933.
Arturo Labriola. *La Guerra di Tripoli e l'Opinione Socialista*. Naples, 1912.
Charles Lapworth. *Tripoli and Young Italy*. London, 1912.
E. Lémonon. "La Lybie et l'Opinion Publique Italienne," in *Questions Diplomatiques et Coloniales,* November 16, 1913, pp. 596 ff.
W. K. McClure. *Italy in North Africa*. Philadelphia, 1914.
Pietro Mamoli. *La Cirenaica*. Naples, 1912.
Federico Minutilli. *Bibliografia della Libia*. Turin, 1903. (Continued by Ugo Ceccherini's work, q.v. in this same section.)
G. Mosca. *Italia e Libia*. Milan, 1912.
C. Muzio. *La Libia*. Venice, 1912.
V. Nazari. *Tripolitania*. Rome, 1912.
P. Nicolas. *Etude sur la Tripolitaine*. Paris, 1904.
Alan Ostler. *The Arabs in Tripoli*. London, 1912.
Guiseppe Piazza. *La Nostra Terra Promessa (Tripolitania)*. Rome, 1911.
Giuseppe Ricchieri. *La Tripolitania e l'Italia*. Milan, 1902.
——————. *Libia Interna*. Rome, 1912.
E. Rouard de Card. *La Politique de la France à l'Egard de la Tripolitaine Pendant le Dernier Siècle*. Toulouse, 1906.
M. Schanz. *Algerien, Tunesien, Tripolitanien*. Halle, 1905.
C. Sforza. *La Tripolitania*. Rome, 1912.
Franco Spada. *La Colonizzazione della Libia*. Bologna, 1914.
M. L. Todd. *Tripoli the Mysterious*. London, 1912.
P. de Vecchi. *Italy's Civilizing Mission in Africa*. Florence, 1912.
A. L. Vischer. "Tripoli: A Land of Little Promise," in *The National Geographic Magazine,* November 1911, pp. 1035 ff.

SOMALILAND

Angelo Cortinois. *La Somalia Italiana.* Milan, 1913.
Giacomo de Martino. *La Somalia Nostra.* Bergamo, 1913.
Vico Mantegazza. *Il Benadir.* Milan, 1908.
Giuseppe Piazza. *Il Benadir.* Rome, 1913.
C. C. Rossetti. *Manuale di Legislazione della Somalia Italiana.* Rome, 1914.
Giorgio Sorrentino. *Ricordi del Benadir.* Naples, 1910.

THE NETHERLANDS COLONIAL EMPIRE

GENERAL

G. K. Anton. *Studien zur Kolonialpolitik der Niederlaender.* Leipzig, 1906.
W. C. Hill. *Select Bibliography of Publications on Foreign Colonisation . . . Dutch (etc.) . . . .* London, 1915.
A. L. Lowell and H. M. Stephens. *Colonial Civil Service . . . in England, Holland and France.* New York, 1900.

THE NETHERLANDS INDIES

Thomas Barbour. "Dutch New Guinea," in *The National Geographic Magazine,* July and August 1908, pp. 469 ff. and 527 ff.
J. M. Brown. *The Dutch East: Sketches and Pictures.* London, 1914.
Antoine Cabaton. *Java, Sumatra and the Other Islands of the Dutch East Indies.* London, 1914.
D. M. Campbell. *Java Past and Present.* 2 vols., London, 1915.
Joseph Chailley-Bert. *Java et ses Habitants.* Paris, 1900.
H. Colijn. *Neërlands Indie: Land en Volk.* 2 vols., Amsterdam, 1911.
Clive Day. *The Dutch in Java.* New York, 1904.
J. de Louter. *Handboek van het Staatsen Administratief Recht van Nederlandsch Indië.* The Hague, 1914.
A. de Wit. *Java.* Philadelphia, 1906.
Pierre Gonnaud. *La Colonisation Hollandaise à Java.* Paris, 1905.
Georges Guyot. *Le Problème de la Main-d'Oeuvre dans les Colonies d'Exploitation: La Côte Est de Sumatra.* Paris, 1910.
H. M. Hiller. "Manners and Customs of the People of Southern Borneo," in *Bulletin of the Geographical Society of Philadelphia,* December 1901, pp. 51 ff.
J. F. Scheltema. "The Opium Traffic in the Dutch East Indies," in *The American Journal of Sociology,* July and September 1907, pp. 79 ff. and 224 ff.
Unsigned. "Explorations in Dutch New Guinea," in *Bulletin of the American Geographical Society,* November 1911, pp. 837 ff.
——————. "Resources of the Dutch East Indies," in *Journal of the American Asiatic Association,* January 1903, pp. 344 ff.
A. S. Walcott. *Java and Her Neighbors.* New York, 1914.

SURINAM AND CURACAO

J. W. D. Aiken. "The Gold Mining Industry in Surinam," in *Timehri,* July 1912, pp. 83 ff.
H. D. Benjamins *et al.*, eds. *Encyclopaedie van Nederlandsch West Indië.* The Hague. Published in parts, 1914-1917, but commonly bound in one volume.
G. P. Blackiston. "The Holland of the Caribbean," in *World Today,* October 1908, pp. 1058 ff.
H. F. Cleland. "Curaçao, a Losing Colonial Venture," in *Bulletin of the American Geographical Society,* March 1909, pp. 125 ff.
H. C. Pearson. "India Rubber in Dutch Guiana," in *The India Rubber World,* January through May 1911, pp. 115 ff., 149 ff., 189 ff., 221 ff. and 257 ff.
J. B. Percival. "The Resources of Dutch Guiana," in *Bulletin of the Pan-American Union,* December 1913, pp. 818 ff.
E. H. Teats. "Notes on Dutch Guiana," in *The Engineering and Mining Journal,* March 24, 1906, pp. 559 ff.
Unsigned. "The Trade of Curaçao," in *The Pan-American Magazine,* September 1914, pp. 52.
J. H. Verloop. *A Brief Outline of the Surinam Gold Industry.* Amsterdam, 1911.

THE PORTUGUESE COLONIAL EMPIRE

GENERAL

A. L. de Almada Negreiros. *Colonies Portugaises.* Lisbon, 1910.
J. H. Harris. *Portuguese Slavery: Britain's Dilemma.* London, 1913.
W. C. Hill. *Select Bibliography of Publications on Foreign Colonisation . . . Portuguese (etc.)* . . . . London, 1915.
Angel Marvaud. *Le Portugal et ses Colonies.* Paris, 1912.
H. W. Nevinson. *A Modern Slavery: Labor in the Portuguese Colonies.* London, 1906.

PORTUGUESE EAST AFRICA (MOZAMBIQUE)

O. W. Barrett. "Impressions and Scenes of Mozambique," in *The National Geographic Magazine,* October 1910, pp. 807 ff.
R. N. Lyne. *Mozambique.* London, 1913.
R. C. F. Maugham. *Portuguese East Africa.* London, 1906.
W. B. Worsfold. *Portuguese Nyassaland.* London, 1899.

PORTUGUESE WEST AFRICA (ANGOLA)

W. A. Cadbury. *Labor in Portuguese West Africa.* London, 1910.
J. J. E. de Lima Vidal. *Por Terras d'Angola.* Coimbra, 1916.
Unsigned. "Angola, the Last Foothold of Slavery," in *The National Geographic Magazine,* July 1910, pp. 625 ff.

ST. THOMAS AND PRINCE'S ISLANDS

H. R. F. Bourne. *Slave Traffic in Portuguese Africa: An Account of Slave-Raiding and Slave-Trading in Angola and of Slavery in the Islands of San Thomé and Principe.* London, 1908.
Unsigned. "The Island of São Thomé," in *Bulletin of the American Geographical Society,* September 1910, pp. 661 ff.

THE RUSSIAN COLONIAL EMPIRE

GENERAL

R. P. Churchill. *The Anglo-Russian Convention of 1907.* Cedar Rapids, 1939.
F. Quadflieg. *Russische Expansionspolitik von 1774 bis 1914.* Berlin, 1914.
Alfred Rambaud. *The Expansion of Russia.* New York, 1904.

ASIATIC RUSSIA

Clarence Cary. "Travel on the Trans-Siberian," in *Journal of the American Asiatic Association,* November 1902, pp. 280 ff.
C. L. Chanler. "The Development of Siberia," in *Journal of the American Asiatic Association,* November 1908, pp. 304 ff.
Colonization Bureau of Russia. *Atlas of Asiatic Russia.* 3 vols., St. Petersburg, 1914.
Jeremiah Curtin. *A Journey in Southern Siberia.* Boston, 1909.
Nelson Fairchild. "Crossing Siberia by Rail," in *Journal of the American Asiatic Association,* February 1907, pp. 19 ff.
Burnett Goodwin. "Via the Trans-Siberian," in *The Four-Track News,* June 1903, pp. 279 ff.
R. T. Greener. "Siberian Trade Notes," in *Journal of the American Asiatic Association,* September 1903, pp. 235 ff.
E. A. Grosvenor. "Siberia," in *The National Geographic Magazine,* September 1901, pp. 317 ff.
Richard Guenther. "The Development of Siberia," in *Journal of the American Asiatic Association,* April 1908, p. 82.
Frederick McCormick. *The Tragedy of Russia in Pacific Asia.* New York, 1904.
H. B. Miller. "Russian Development of Manchuria," in *The National Geographic Magazine,* March 1904, pp. 113 ff.
L. O. Packard. "Russian Expansion and the Long Struggle for Open Ports," in *The Journal of Geography,* October 1913, pp. 33 ff.
H. G. Perry-Ayscough and R. B. Otter-Barry. *With the Russians in Mongolia.* London, 1914.
M. P. Price. *Siberia.* New York, 1912.

Paul Rohrbach. *Die russische Weltmacht in Mittel und Westasien.* Leipzig, 1904.
M. M. Shoemaker. *The Great Siberian Railway.* New York, 1903.
Unsigned. *Aziatskaia Rossiia.* 3 vols., St. Petersburg, 1914.
——————. "The Cost of the Trans-Siberian Railway," in *Journal of the American Asiatic Association,* September 1902, pp. 216 ff.
——————. "England and Russia in Central Asia," in *Journal of the American Asiatic Association,* March 1909, pp. 42 ff.
——————. "The Partition of Sakhalin," in *Bulletin of the American Geographical Society,* December 1905, pp. 724 ff.
——————. "Russia as a Pacific Power," in *Journal of the American Asiatic Association,* July 1903, pp. 181 ff.
——————. "Russian Ports in the Far East," in *Journal of the American Asiatic Association,* September 1912, p. 244.
A. Woeikof. *Le Turkestan Russe.* Paris, 1914.
G. F. Wright. *Asiatic Russia.* 2 vols., London, 1903.

THE SPANISH COLONIAL EMPIRE

GENERAL

F. E. Chadwick. *The Relations of the United States and Spain: The Spanish-American War.* 2 vols., New York, 1911.
Frederick Funston. *Memories of Two Wars: Cuban and Philippine Experiences.* New York, 1911.
José Yanguas Messia. *Apuntes sobre la Expansión Colonial en Africa.* Madrid, 1915.
J. W. Pratt. *The [American] Expansionists of 1898: The Acquisition of Hawaii and the Spanish Islands.* Baltimore, 1936.
J. W. Root. *Spain and Its Colonies.* London, 1898.
L. M. Sears. "French Opinion of the Spanish-American War," in *The Hispanic American Historical Review,* February 1927, pp. 25 ff.
L. B. Shippee. "Germany and the Spanish-American War," in *The American Historical Review,* July 1925, pp. 574 ff.
M. M. Wilkerson. *Public Opinion and the Spanish-American War.* Baton Rouge, 1932.
H. W. Wilson. *The Downfall of Spain.* London, 1900.

CUBA

W. F. Johnson. *A History of Cuba.* 5 vols., New York, 1920.
A. G. Robinson. *Cuba and the Intervention.* New York, 1905.
Theodore Roosevelt. *The Rough Riders.* New York, 1899.

THE PHILIPPINES

T. A. Bailey. "Dewey and the Germans at Manila Bay," in *The American Historical Review,* October 1939, pp. 59 ff.
D. P. Barrows. "The Governor-General of the Philippines under Spain and the United States," in *The American Historical Review,* January 1916, pp. 288 ff.
L. H. Fernández. *A Brief History of the Philippines.* Boston, 1919.
P. F. Jernegan. *A Short History of the Philippines.* New York, 1905.
M. M. Kalaw. *The Development of Philippine Politics, 1872-1920.* Manila, 1927.

PUERTO RICO

R. A. van Middeldyk. *A History of Puerto Rico.* New York, 1903.

SPANISH MOROCCO

Jerónimo Bécker. *Historia de Marruecos.* Madrid, 1915.
Emilio Bueno y Nuñez de Prado. *Historia de la Acción de España en Marruecos.* Madrid, 1929.
E. P. Corredor. *Historia de la Zona del Protectorado de España en el Norte de Marruecos.* Madrid, 1933.
Alfonso Merry del Val. "The Spanish Zones in Morocco," in *The Geographical Journal,* May and June 1920, pp. 329 ff. and 409 ff.

THE WEST AFRICAN POSSESSIONS

Julio Arija. *La Guinea Española y sus Riquezas.* Madrid, 1930.

P. de Cénival and F. de la Chapelle. "Possessions Espagnoles sur la Côte Occidentale d'Afrique," in *Hésperis*, 1935, pp. 19 ff.
Great Britain. Foreign Office. *Spanish Sahara*. London, 1920.
R. Peyronnet. "Sud-Ouest Marocain, Rio de Oro et Sahara Occidental," in *Bulletin de la Société de Géographie d'Alger et de l'Afrique du Nord*, 1928, pp. 687 ff.

NEAR EASTERN RIVALRIES
GENERAL

C. H. Becker. *Deutschland und der Islam*. Berlin, 1914.
André Brisse. "Les Intérêts de l'Allemagne dans l'Empire Ottoman," in *Revue de Géographie*, March through June 1902, pp. 185 ff., 294 ff., 386 ff. and 484 ff.
T. G. Djuvara. *Cent Projets de Partage de la Turquie, 1281-1913*. Paris, 1914.
Hugo Grothe. *Deutschland, die Turkei und der Islam*. Leipzig, 1914.
Ellsworth Huntington. *Palestine and Its Transformation*. Boston, 1911.
——————. "Railroads in Asia Minor," in *Bulletin of the American Geographical Society*, November 1909, pp. 691 ff.
M. E. W. Latimer. *Russia and Turkey in the Nineteenth Century*. Chicago, 1905.
Alfons Raab. *Die Politik Deutschlands im Nahen Orient von 1878-1908*. Vienna, 1936.
M. W. Tyler. *The European Powers and the Near East, 1875-1908*. Minneapolis, 1925.
Hans Uebersberger. *Russlands Orientpolitik in den letzten zwei Jahrhunderten*. Stuttgart, 1913.
Noel Verney and George Dambmann. *Les Puissances Etrangères dans le Levant, en Syrie et en Palestine*. Paris, 1900.
C. M. Watson. *Fifty Years' Work in the Holy Land . . . . 1865-1915*. London, 1915.

MIDDLE EASTERN RIVALRIES
GENERAL

Ewald Banse. *Auf den Spuren der Bagdadbahn*. Weimar, 1913.
André Chéradame. *Le Chemin de Fer de Bagdad*. Paris, 1915.
Valentine Chirol. *The Middle Eastern Question*. London, 1903.
H. A. Gibbons. *The New Map of Asia, 1900-1919*. New York, 1919.
Angus Hamilton. *Problems of the Middle East*. London, 1909.
Georges Mazel. *Le Chemin de Fer de Bagdad*. Montpellier, 1911.
Louis Ragey. *La Question du Chemin de Fer de Bagdad, 1893-1914*. Paris, 1936.
Paul Rohrbach. *Die Bagdadbahn*. Berlin, 1911.
Arthur von Gwinner. "The Bagdad Railway and the Question of British Cooperation," in *The Nineteenth Century*, June 1909, pp. 1083 ff.

AFGHANISTAN

W. A. Clark. "Afghanistan," in *Journal of the American Asiatic Association*, September 1907, pp. 245 ff.
Ellsworth Huntington. "The Relation of Afghanistan to Its Neighbors," in *Bulletin of the Geographical Society of Philadelphia*, October 1908, pp. 1 ff.
G. Lyons. *Afghanistan: The Buffer State*. London, 1910.
Mir Munshi. *The Constitution and Laws of Afghanistan*. London, 1910.
Frank Noyce. *England, India and Afghanistan*. London, 1902.
G. P. Tate. *The Kingdom of Afghanistan*. London, 1911.

ARABIA

N. Azoury. *Le Réveil de la Nation Arabe dans l'Asie Turque*. Paris, 1905.
D. G. Hogarth. *The Penetration of Arabia*. New York, 1904.

PERSIA

Victor Bérard. *Révolutions de la Perse*. Paris, 1910.
E. G. Browne. *The Persian Revolution of 1905-1909*. Cambridge, 1910.
R. P. Churchill. *The Anglo-Russian Convention of 1907*. Cedar Rapids, 1939.
David Fraser. *Persia and Turkey in Revolt*. London, 1910.
J. M. Hone. *Persia in Revolution*. London, 1910.
A. V. W. Jackson. *Persia Past and Present*. New York, 1909.
W. M. Shuster. *The Strangling of Persia*. New York, 1912.
Bernard Temple. *The Place of Persia in World Politics*. London, 1910.

THIBET

Edmund Candler. *The Unveiling of Lhasa.* London, 1905.
H. H. P. Deasy. *In Thibet and Chinese Turkestan.* New York, 1901.
Sven Hedin. *Adventures in Thibet.* London, 1904.
——————. *Central Asia and Thibet Towards the Holy City of Lhasa.* 2 vols., London, 1903.
——————. *Trans-Himalaya: Discoveries and Adventures in Thibet.* 3 vols., London, 1909-1913.
T. H. Holdich. *Thibet the Mysterious.* New York, 1906.
P. Landon. *The Opening of Thibet.* New York, 1905.
Unsigned. "Explorations in Thibet," in *The National Geographic Magazine,* September 1903, pp. 353 ff.
——————. "Treaty Obligations in Thibet," in *Journal of the American Asiatic Association,* November 1912, pp. 306 ff.
L. A. Waddell. *Lhasa and Its Mysteries . . . .* London, 1905.
Francis Younghusband. *India and Thibet.* London, 1910.

FAR EASTERN RIVALRIES

GENERAL

N. Ariga. *La Guerre Russo-Japonaise.* Paris, 1908.
Kanichi Asakawa. "The Japanese in Southern Manchuria," in *Journal of the American Asiatic Association,* February 1911, pp. 17 ff.
——————. *The Russo-Japanese Conflict.* Boston, 1904.
Otto Becker. *Der Ferne-Osten und das Schicksals Europas, 1907-1918.* Leipzig, 1940.
André Chéradame. *Le Monde et la Guerre Russo-Japonaise.* Paris, 1906.
F. D. Cloud. "Agriculture in Manchuria," in *Journal of the American Asiatic Association,* May 1909, pp. 111 ff.
P. H. Clyde. *International Rivalries in Manchuria, 1689-1922.* Columbus, 1930.
A. L. P. Dennis. *The Anglo-Japanese Alliance.* Berkeley, 1923.
Edouard Driault. *La Question d'Extrême-Orient.* Paris, 1908.
F. D. Fisher. "Manchurian Trade and Commerce," in *Journal of the American Asiatic Association,* December 1911, pp. 334 ff.
——————. "Trade in Manchuria," in *Journal of the American Asiatic Association,* March 1911, pp. 55 ff.
Otto Franke. *Die Grossmaechte in Ostasien von 1894 bis 1914.* Brunswick, 1923.
Great Britain. Historical Section of the Committee of Imperial Defence. *Official History, Naval and Military, of the Russo-Japanese War.* 3 vols., London, 1910-1920.
A. S. Hershey. *The International Law and Diplomacy of the Russo-Japanese War.* New York, 1906.
S. K. Hornbeck. *Contemporary Politics in the Far East.* New York, 1916.
T. Hoshino. *The Economic History of Manchuria.* Seoul, 1920.
George Kennan. "E. H. Harriman's Imperial Project: A Notable Plan to Control the Trans-Siberian Railway," in *Asia,* June 1917, pp. 271 ff.
A. N. Kuropatkin. *The Russian Army and the Japanese War.* 2 vols., London, 1909.
J. Lionel. *The War in the Far East, 1904-1905.* London, 1905.
H. B. Miller. "Russian Development of Manchuria," in *The National Geographic Magazine,* March 1904, pp. 113 ff.
Gotaro Ogawa. *Expenditures of the Russo-Japanese War.* New York, 1923.
René Pinon. *La Lutte pour le Pacifique: Origine et Résultats de la Guerre Russo-Japonaise.* Paris, 1906.
E. B. Price. *The Russo-Japanese Treaties of 1907-1916 Concerning Manchuria and Mongolia.* Baltimore, 1933.
F. Quadflieg. *Russische Expansionspolitik von 1774 bis 1914.* Berlin, 1914.
Charles Ross. *The Russo-Japanese War, 1904-1905.* New York, 1912.
M. E. Stone. "Race Prejudice in the Far East," in *The National Geographic Magazine,* December 1910, pp. 973 ff.
W. G. Swartz. "Anglo-Russian Rivalry in the Far East, 1895-1905," in *The University of Iowa Studies,* December 1, 1932, pp. 158 ff.

Unsigned. "Commercial Neutralization of the Railways in Manchuria," in *Journal of the American Asiatic Association,* February 1910, pp. 4 ff.
—————. "Japan's Railway Problems in Manchuria," in *Journal of the American Asiatic Association,* October 1906, pp. 266.
—————. "New Railways in North Manchuria," in *Journal of the American Asiatic Association,* July 1916, pp. 181 ff.
—————. "Russia's Aim in the Far East," in *Journal of the American Asiatic Association,* April 1914, pp. 83 ff.
—————. "Russian Ports in the Far East," in *Journal of the American Asiatic Association,* September 1912, p. 244.
—————. "The South Manchurian Railway," in *Journal of the American Asiatic Association,* March 1908 and July 1909, pp. 54 and 178 ff.
E. T. Williams. "The Open Ports of China," in *The Geographical Review,* April-May-June 1920, pp. 306 ff.
Ernst zu Reventlow. *Der Russisch-Japanische Kreig.* 2 vols., Berlin, 1905-1906.

NOV 12
DUE

DARTMOUTH COLLEGE
3 3311 01023 1944